Fight, Fight, Fight – The Unyielding Legacy

Part I: The Rise of Donald J. Trump

Chapter 1: Entering the Political Arena

Donald J. Trump's journey into the American political landscape was as unexpected as it was dramatic. Before becoming a household name in politics, Trump was primarily recognized as a real estate mogul, reality television star, and public figure. His entry into politics marked a significant turning point, both for himself and for American political culture.

Early Life and Business Ventures

Trump was born on June 14, 1946, in Queens, New York City. The son of real estate developer Fred Trump, Donald grew up in a business-focused environment, which heavily influenced his early career choices. After graduating from the Wharton School of the University of Pennsylvania in 1968, he joined his father's real estate business. Initially concentrating on middle-income housing projects in Brooklyn and Queens, Trump soon set his sights on Manhattan's more lucrative real estate market.

Through the 1970s and 1980s, Trump became synonymous with high-stakes real estate deals, developing iconic properties such as the Grand Hyatt New York, Trump Tower on Fifth Avenue, and the Trump Plaza Hotel and Casino in Atlantic City. His business ventures were not limited to real estate; he also ventured into various industries, including casinos, airlines, and even professional football with the United States Football League (USFL). Despite ups and downs, including multiple bankruptcies, Trump's name became synonymous with luxury and bold branding, laying the groundwork for his celebrity status.

Decision to Run for President

By the early 2000s, Trump's presence had grown beyond real estate; he had become a television icon through his reality show, The Apprentice, which aired from 2004 to 2015. This exposure brought Trump closer to the average American viewer, allowing him to present himself as a no-nonsense, business-savvy figure who could "make deals" and "fire" those who failed to meet expectations.

Trump had flirted with the idea of running for president as early as the late 1980s, but his official entry into the political arena did not occur until June 16, 2015, when he announced his candidacy for the 2016 presidential election. The announcement, made in the lobby of Trump Tower, sent shockwaves through the political establishment. Trump's campaign launch speech centered around a promise to "Make America Great Again," a slogan that would become central to his political identity. He emphasized issues like illegal immigration, trade imbalances, and job losses, connecting with a segment of the American electorate that felt ignored by traditional politicians.

Key Campaign Strategies

From the outset, Trump's campaign defied conventional political wisdom. Unlike most candidates, who relied heavily on professional campaign consultants, Trump trusted his instincts and embraced an unfiltered approach to communication. He frequently bypassed traditional media outlets, using social media, particularly Twitter, as his primary means of reaching the public. His tweets were often controversial, but they resonated with his supporters, who appreciated his directness and willingness to challenge the status quo.

Trump's campaign was marked by fiery rallies that attracted large crowds, often in key swing states. His speeches were filled with promises to build a wall along the U.S.-Mexico border, renegotiate trade agreements, and bring back manufacturing jobs. His approach, which some saw as blunt and others as refreshingly honest, polarized the electorate. His critics accused him of fostering division, while his supporters viewed him as a champion of the "forgotten man" who was not afraid to speak the truth.

As the Republican primary progressed, Trump's opponents, including seasoned politicians like Jeb Bush, Ted Cruz, and Marco Rubio, struggled to counter his unorthodox campaign style. He dominated the debates with quick comebacks, often branding his opponents with nicknames that stuck, such as "Low-Energy Jeb" and "Lyin' Ted." His ability to dominate media coverage, coupled with his appeal to a base that felt increasingly disenfranchised, helped him secure the Republican nomination in July 2016.

Trump's entry into the political arena was a seismic shift in American politics, challenging long-held assumptions about what it takes to win a presidential election. His rise to prominence would set the tone for a tumultuous and transformative era in U.S. politics.

Chapter 2: The 2016 Presidential Campaign

When Donald J. Trump officially declared his candidacy in mid-2015, many political analysts dismissed his bid as a publicity stunt or, at best, a long shot. However, Trump would soon prove to be a formidable contender, turning the 2016 presidential campaign into one of the most unpredictable and polarizing races in modern American history. His journey from outsider to victor reshaped the Republican Party and the broader political landscape.

Primary Battles

The 2016 Republican primary was crowded, with 17 candidates vying for the nomination. Among them were seasoned politicians like Jeb Bush, Marco Rubio, Ted Cruz, and John Kasich, as well as figures like Ben Carson and Carly Fiorina. Despite their political credentials, Trump managed to dominate the crowded field with a brash, unfiltered style that appealed to a broad swath of disillusioned voters. From the beginning, Trump's strategy focused on positioning himself as an outsider who could shake up Washington, contrasting sharply with the "establishment" candidates he faced.

Throughout the primaries, Trump's campaign events were marked by high energy, large crowds, and often controversial statements. He made headlines by proposing a temporary ban on Muslim immigration, calling for stronger border enforcement, and questioning long-standing trade deals like NAFTA. His rallies became raucous affairs, drawing both passionate supporters and vocal protesters. The media's fascination with Trump, combined with his ability to create sound bites that quickly went viral, allowed him to outshine his competitors in both traditional and digital media coverage.

Trump's dominance in the primaries was cemented with key wins in states like New Hampshire, South Carolina, and Nevada. As his competitors dropped out one by one, the race ultimately came down to Trump and Texas Senator Ted Cruz. Despite Cruz's strong showing among evangelical voters, Trump's broader appeal and media mastery allowed him to secure the necessary delegates to clinch the nomination. In a dramatic turn of events, Trump officially accepted the Republican nomination at the Republican National Convention in Cleveland in July 2016, delivering a speech that emphasized themes of law and order, economic growth, and national sovereignty.

Defying the Odds in the General Election

The general election battle between Trump and Democratic nominee Hillary Clinton was intense, marked by stark contrasts in style, policy, and vision for the country. Clinton, a seasoned politician and former Secretary of State, represented experience and continuity, while Trump presented himself as the outsider who would "drain the swamp." The clash between the two candidates highlighted deep divisions in the American electorate.

From the outset, Clinton was widely seen as the favorite to win. Her campaign had a significant advantage in funding, organization, and endorsements. Most polls showed her leading Trump, sometimes by significant margins. However, Trump's unconventional approach continued to shake up the race. He focused on swing states that had traditionally leaned Democratic, such as Pennsylvania, Wisconsin, and Michigan, sensing an opportunity to tap into working-class voters who felt left behind by globalization and economic changes.

Despite multiple controversies that emerged during the campaign—including Trump's comments about women on a leaked Access Hollywood tape and Clinton's ongoing email server investigation—both candidates continued to drive forward. Trump capitalized on issues like immigration, trade, and national security, while Clinton emphasized healthcare, women's rights, and gun control. The debates between the two candidates were fiery and personal, reflecting the high stakes of the election.

The night of November 8, 2016, defied the expectations of political pundits and pollsters. As the results rolled in, Trump managed to secure crucial victories in key swing states, capturing enough Electoral College votes to win the presidency. His victory was a stunning upset, widely viewed as a referendum on the establishment and the mainstream media. Trump's unexpected triumph signified not just a win for his campaign but a seismic shift in American politics, as traditional voting patterns were upended.

Media Battles and Social Media Strategy

Throughout the 2016 campaign, Trump's relationship with the media was both symbiotic and adversarial. While his unorthodox behavior and polarizing statements drew extensive media coverage, Trump frequently criticized major news outlets, calling them "fake news" and accusing them of bias. This antagonistic relationship with the media played a central role in Trump's campaign narrative, as he positioned himself as fighting against a media elite that he claimed was biased against ordinary Americans.

Trump's use of social media, particularly Twitter, became a defining feature of his campaign. He used it not only to communicate directly with his supporters but also to shape media coverage. His tweets were often provocative, sparking debates and garnering headlines. Trump's ability to bypass traditional media filters allowed him to control the narrative and energize his base. His supporters saw him as authentic and relatable, even if his style was sometimes coarse.

Trump also made effective use of other digital platforms. His campaign utilized targeted online advertising, data analytics, and social media campaigns to mobilize voters. The campaign's use of Facebook to micro-target potential voters, particularly in swing states, proved to be highly effective, reaching segments of the electorate that had previously been overlooked by traditional campaigns.

The 2016 presidential campaign was a watershed moment, marking the rise of populist politics, the power of digital media, and a fundamental shift in how candidates communicate with voters. Trump's victory demonstrated that a candidate who understood media dynamics and voter sentiment could overcome significant odds, even in the face of well-funded opposition.

Chapter 3: The Unexpected Win

Donald Trump's victory in the 2016 presidential election was one of the most dramatic moments in modern American politics. While Trump's campaign had consistently defied expectations, few anticipated the scale of his eventual win, especially against a seasoned opponent like Hillary Clinton.

Election Night Shock

On November 8, 2016, election night began with a sense of cautious optimism at Hillary Clinton's campaign headquarters, while Trump's team prepared for what many thought would be a concession. As initial results came in from states like Virginia and North Carolina, Clinton held a slight lead, fueling confidence among her supporters. However, as the night progressed, key swing states such as Florida, Ohio, and Pennsylvania leaned toward Trump, sparking shockwaves across newsrooms and campaign war rooms.

The most significant surprises of the night came from the Rust Belt states. Despite polling that had shown Clinton ahead, Trump managed to secure victories in Pennsylvania, Michigan, and Wisconsin—states that had not voted Republican since the 1980s. The final tipping point came when Trump was declared the winner of Pennsylvania, pushing him past the 270 electoral votes needed to secure the presidency. Clinton had won the popular vote by nearly three million votes, but Trump's strategic focus on the Electoral College, particularly in working-class regions, proved decisive.

The mood at Clinton's campaign headquarters turned from hopeful anticipation to stunned disbelief. Many of her supporters were visibly emotional, grappling with a loss that seemed improbable just hours earlier. Trump, meanwhile, delivered his victory speech in the early hours of the morning, striking a surprisingly conciliatory tone and pledging to be a president for "all Americans."

The shock of Trump's win was felt not only in the United States but globally, as world leaders and international markets scrambled to understand what his presidency might mean for the global order. His unexpected victory underscored a deep discontent among American voters and marked a turning point in U.S. politics, with populism taking center stage.

The Transition to the Presidency

After the initial shock of his victory, Trump faced the complex task of transitioning from the campaign trail to the White House. The transition period was marked by a series of high-profile meetings at Trump Tower, where he interviewed potential cabinet members and advisors. Trump's choices for his administration signaled a break from political norms, as he selected individuals from the business world, the military, and even some former political rivals.

One of Trump's most controversial appointments was Steve Bannon as Chief Strategist, sparking intense debate over Bannon's connections to the alt-right. Other appointments, such as Rex Tillerson as Secretary of State and Jeff Sessions as Attorney General, reinforced Trump's focus on appointing figures aligned with his "America First" agenda.

Trump's decision to maintain control of his business empire during his presidency drew significant criticism over potential conflicts of interest. Despite this, he continued to press forward with his policy agenda, using Twitter as a primary means of communication with the American public. His unfiltered tweets often set the day's news agenda, a strategy that kept the media focused on him while maintaining direct contact with his base.

Inauguration Day, January 20, 2017, marked the official beginning of Trump's presidency. His inaugural address reinforced many of the themes that had defined his campaign, particularly nationalism, economic revival, and a promise to return power to the people. Trump's speech was stark, painting a picture of a nation plagued by crime, economic decay, and failed leadership, but one that could be restored under his administration. It was a defining moment, setting the tone for what would become one of the most unconventional presidencies in American history.

Analyzing Trump's Coalition

Trump's coalition of voters was complex and diverse, revealing unexpected alliances that defied traditional political boundaries. At the heart of his support were white, working-class voters who had felt increasingly alienated by globalization, automation, and changing social norms. These voters, many of whom resided in the industrial Midwest, were drawn to Trump's message of economic nationalism and his promises to revive American manufacturing.

Trump also found strong support among evangelical Christians, despite his unconventional personal life and lack of a deep religious background. Evangelicals rallied behind Trump largely because of his commitments to conservative Supreme Court appointments, pro-life policies, and religious liberty protections. His rhetoric on issues like immigration, law and order, and national security further resonated with this group.

Another critical aspect of Trump's coalition was the "forgotten man"—voters who felt left behind by economic changes, neglected by the political establishment, and ignored by coastal elites. Trump's populist message, which emphasized a rejection of political correctness, resonated strongly with these voters, who saw him as an unfiltered voice of their frustrations.

Trump's ability to win over suburban and rural voters, coupled with his appeal among white voters without college degrees, was crucial in securing his victory. His campaign capitalized on Clinton's weaknesses, particularly her "basket of deplorables" comment, which many Trump supporters viewed as emblematic of elite disdain for ordinary Americans.

In addition to demographic factors, Trump's success was driven by his strategic focus on the Electoral College. He prioritized swing states and regions where he could flip key counties that had previously leaned Democratic. This strategic approach, combined with his ability to mobilize voter turnout in crucial areas, allowed him to build a winning coalition despite losing the popular vote.

Trump's unexpected win in 2016 was not just a political upset; it was a reconfiguration of the American electorate, highlighting deep economic, cultural, and political divides. His coalition reflected a broader realignment, bringing together voters who felt abandoned by both parties and energized by a candidate who promised to disrupt the status quo.

Part II: The First Term – Triumphs and Challenges

Chapter 4: Promises Kept and Broken

Donald Trump's first term as president was characterized by a series of ambitious policy initiatives that reflected his campaign promises. His administration sought to tackle a broad range of issues, from tax reform and economic growth to immigration and healthcare. While some of his promises were fulfilled, others faced significant challenges and resistance.

Tax Cuts and Economic Growth

One of Trump's earliest and most significant legislative achievements was the passage of the Tax Cuts and Jobs Act of 2017. This landmark piece of legislation aimed to stimulate economic growth by reducing the corporate tax rate from 35% to 21%, the largest reduction in decades. The act also included tax cuts for individuals, though these were temporary and scheduled to phase out by 2025. Proponents of the tax cuts argued that they would encourage businesses to invest, hire more workers, and increase wages. Critics, however, contended that the cuts disproportionately benefited the wealthy and large corporations, leading to an increase in the federal deficit.

In the years following the tax reform, the economy experienced significant growth, with GDP rising and unemployment rates dropping to record lows. Job creation remained strong, particularly in manufacturing, retail, and construction sectors, which had been key focal points of Trump's campaign. Trump frequently touted these economic gains, attributing them to his administration's policies of deregulation, energy expansion, and tax cuts.

However, the economic boom was not without controversy. While Wall Street experienced a surge, wage growth for middle and lower-income workers lagged behind. Trump's critics argued that the benefits of the tax cuts were skewed toward the wealthiest Americans, with stock buybacks and corporate profits increasing more than worker wages. Additionally, the federal deficit rose significantly, prompting concerns about long-term fiscal sustainability. Despite these criticisms, Trump and his administration maintained that the economic growth under his presidency represented a promise kept to the American people.

Immigration Policies and Border Security

From the beginning, Trump's presidency was marked by a strong focus on immigration reform and border security, both of which had been central themes of his campaign. One of his first actions as president was to sign an executive order restricting travel from several predominantly Muslim countries, a move that sparked widespread protests and legal challenges. The "travel ban," as it was commonly known, was revised multiple times before finally being upheld by the Supreme Court in 2018.

Trump also took a hardline stance on border security, emphasizing the need to build a wall along the U.S.-Mexico border. Funding for the wall became a major point of contention between the Trump administration and Congress, leading to a government shutdown in early 2019. Despite these hurdles, Trump redirected funds from the Defense Department to construct parts of the border wall, framing it as a fulfillment of his campaign pledge to secure America's borders.

The administration also implemented a controversial "zero tolerance" policy at the border, which led to the separation of migrant families and drew sharp criticism from both domestic and international human rights organizations. The images of children held in detention facilities became a flashpoint in national debates over immigration policy. Trump defended the policy as a necessary measure to enforce the law and deter illegal immigration, while opponents argued that it violated human rights and represented a broken promise to uphold American values of compassion and justice.

Trump's immigration policies also included attempts to end the Deferred Action for Childhood Arrivals (DACA) program, which protected undocumented immigrants who had arrived in the U.S. as children. While the administration argued that DACA was an overreach of executive authority, efforts to terminate the program were blocked by the Supreme Court in a landmark ruling in 2020. Immigration reform remained a divisive issue throughout Trump's presidency, with significant promises kept, but also challenges and partial reversals along the way.

Health Care and the Challenges of Repealing Obamacare

Repealing and replacing the Affordable Care Act (ACA), commonly known as Obamacare, was one of Trump's most prominent campaign promises. He criticized the ACA as a failure, citing rising insurance premiums and limited choices for consumers. The effort to dismantle Obamacare became a major legislative priority for Trump and the Republican-controlled Congress during his first year in office.

In 2017, House Republicans passed the American Health Care Act (AHCA), which aimed to repeal significant portions of the ACA. The bill proposed eliminating the individual mandate, reducing Medicaid expansion, and allowing states more flexibility in regulating insurance. However, the AHCA faced fierce opposition from Democrats and even some moderate Republicans who were concerned about the impact on coverage for individuals with pre-existing conditions and low-income Americans.

The Senate's attempt to pass healthcare reform was fraught with drama, culminating in a narrow defeat when Senator John McCain, in a dramatic late-night vote, gave a "thumbs down" to the repeal bill. The failure to repeal Obamacare was a major setback for Trump, who had promised voters a quick and comprehensive overhaul of the healthcare system.

Despite the setback, Trump continued to make efforts to undermine the ACA through executive actions, including reducing funding for outreach and enrollment, and expanding access to short-term insurance plans that did not meet ACA requirements. His administration also supported a lawsuit led by Republican state attorneys general that aimed to declare the ACA unconstitutional. While the lawsuit remained unresolved during Trump's first term, healthcare remained a key issue for his administration, representing both a significant challenge and an unfulfilled promise.

In sum, Trump's first term was marked by notable policy victories and significant setbacks. His administration's efforts to fulfill campaign promises on tax reform, immigration, and healthcare were met with both success and fierce resistance. While Trump's supporters viewed these efforts as evidence of his commitment to change, his critics saw them as emblematic of an administration that was often at odds with traditional American values and governance norms.

Chapter 5: The Russia Investigation

Donald Trump's first term was heavily overshadowed by the Russia investigation, a complex and highly charged inquiry that raised questions about foreign interference, potential collusion, and the integrity of American democracy. The investigation, which began before Trump's inauguration, became a defining issue of his presidency and a focal point of partisan battles in Washington.

Allegations of Collusion

The Russia investigation was sparked by allegations that members of Trump's campaign had coordinated with Russian operatives to influence the outcome of the 2016 election. These allegations emerged after the U.S. intelligence community concluded that Russia had interfered in the election through a series of hacking and disinformation campaigns designed to sow discord and weaken Clinton's candidacy. The investigation centered on whether Trump's campaign had colluded with the Russian government to secure his victory.

Several events intensified suspicions of collusion. Among the most significant was the June 2016 meeting at Trump Tower between top campaign officials, including Donald Trump Jr., Jared Kushner, and then-campaign chairman Paul Manafort, and a Russian lawyer who allegedly promised damaging information about Clinton. This meeting became a key point of interest for investigators, as it suggested a potential willingness to accept help from a foreign power.

Other incidents included Manafort's prior business dealings with pro-Russian figures in Ukraine, Michael Flynn's discussions with the Russian ambassador about sanctions, and Trump's public call for Russia to find Clinton's "missing emails" during a campaign rally. These events, coupled with reports of frequent contacts between campaign aides and Russian officials, fueled speculation and media coverage of a possible conspiracy.

The investigation gained momentum when Trump abruptly fired FBI Director James Comey in May 2017. Comey later testified before Congress, claiming that Trump had asked him to drop an investigation into Flynn, who had resigned as National Security Advisor after lying about his contacts with the Russian ambassador. The firing of Comey led to the appointment of Special Counsel Robert Mueller, a former FBI director, to oversee the investigation.

Mueller Report Outcomes

Robert Mueller's investigation, which lasted nearly two years, was one of the most high-profile and scrutinized inquiries in U.S. history. The special counsel's team conducted extensive interviews, reviewed documents, and brought charges against several individuals associated with Trump's campaign, including Manafort, Flynn, and Roger Stone. While these charges primarily focused on financial crimes, lying to investigators, and obstruction of justice, they did not establish a clear conspiracy between the Trump campaign and Russian operatives.

The long-awaited Mueller Report, released in April 2019, was a two-part document detailing the findings of the investigation. The first part addressed Russian interference in the 2016 election, confirming that the Russian government had carried out a sweeping campaign of cyberattacks and disinformation. It also described numerous contacts between Trump's associates and Russian officials but concluded that there was insufficient evidence to prove a criminal conspiracy or coordination.

The second part of the report focused on potential obstruction of justice by President Trump. Mueller's team outlined ten instances where Trump had allegedly attempted to interfere with the investigation, including efforts to limit its scope, pressure witnesses, and encourage officials to dismiss Mueller. While the report did not explicitly accuse Trump of a crime, it did not exonerate him either. Mueller stated that if they had been able to clear the president of wrongdoing, they would have said so.

The release of the Mueller Report was met with fierce reactions from both sides of the political spectrum. Democrats viewed it as evidence of Trump's unethical behavior and a potential basis for impeachment, while Republicans claimed it vindicated Trump by failing to prove collusion or obstruction beyond a reasonable doubt. Attorney General William Barr's summary of the report, which stated that Trump had not colluded with Russia or obstructed justice, further fueled the controversy, with critics accusing Barr of downplaying Mueller's findings.

Trump's Defense Strategy

Throughout the investigation, Trump consistently maintained his innocence, describing the Russia inquiry as a "witch hunt" orchestrated by his political enemies to undermine his presidency. His defense strategy was aggressive and multi-faceted, involving direct attacks on Mueller, Comey, and the "deep state," as well as a broader campaign to discredit the investigation in the eyes of the public.

Trump's most effective defense tactic was his use of social media, particularly Twitter, where he regularly criticized the investigation, labeled it a hoax, and portrayed himself as a victim of a partisan plot. His unrelenting rhetoric galvanized his supporters, many of whom saw the investigation as an attempt by establishment forces to delegitimize a duly elected president. This narrative resonated strongly with Trump's base, reinforcing their support and skepticism of the mainstream media.

Legally, Trump's team of lawyers, including Rudy Giuliani, Jay Sekulow, and others, adopted a strategy of non-cooperation, limiting access to documents and witnesses while asserting executive privilege where possible. This approach aimed to slow down the investigation and prevent potentially damaging revelations. Trump himself refused to sit for an in-person interview with Mueller's team, providing written answers instead, which limited the special counsel's ability to assess his credibility directly.

Trump's defense strategy extended to the media, with surrogates appearing frequently on cable news to promote the narrative of a politically motivated investigation. Fox News, in particular, played a crucial role in shaping public opinion, often portraying Mueller's team as biased and unfair.

Ultimately, the Russia investigation concluded without criminal charges against Trump, but it left lasting scars on his presidency and further polarized an already divided nation. It fueled calls for impeachment among Democrats and deepened the distrust between Trump and the intelligence community. For Trump and his supporters, it became a symbol of his battle against the establishment, a fight he framed as central to his political identity and agenda.

Chapter 6: Impeachment Attempt

Donald Trump's presidency faced one of its most critical challenges in 2019, when a phone call with Ukrainian President Volodymyr Zelensky led to his impeachment by the House of Representatives. This marked only the third time in U.S. history that a president had been impeached, setting the stage for a high-stakes political showdown.

The Ukraine Controversy

The controversy began in July 2019, when Trump spoke with President Zelensky and allegedly pressured him to investigate Joe Biden, a potential rival in the 2020 presidential election, and his son, Hunter Biden, who had business dealings in Ukraine. According to a whistleblower's complaint and testimony from administration officials, Trump's request was linked to the withholding of nearly $400 million in military aid to

Ukraine, which was fighting Russian-backed separatists in the Donbas region. The allegation that Trump sought a "quid pro quo"—a favor in exchange for aid—was at the center of the impeachment inquiry.

The phone call became public in September 2019, following the whistleblower complaint that described Trump's actions as an abuse of power. The release of a partial transcript of the call by the White House fueled further scrutiny, as it appeared to confirm that Trump had asked Zelensky to "do us a favor" by launching investigations. Trump's critics argued that this was a clear attempt to solicit foreign interference in the upcoming election, violating both ethical norms and national security interests.

The impeachment inquiry, led by House Democrats, focused on whether Trump's conduct constituted abuse of power and obstruction of Congress. The hearings featured testimonies from officials such as Ambassador Bill Taylor, former U.S. Ambassador to Ukraine Marie Yovanovitch, and National Security Council aide Lt. Col. Alexander Vindman. These testimonies portrayed a concerted effort by Trump and his allies, including Rudy Giuliani, to pressure Ukraine into announcing investigations that could politically benefit Trump.

Trump and his defenders denied any wrongdoing, arguing that his request was part of an effort to combat corruption in Ukraine. They also claimed that there was no explicit linkage between the military aid and the requested investigations, dismissing the controversy as another attempt by Democrats to undermine Trump's presidency. The phrase "No Quid Pro Quo," frequently used by Trump, became a rallying cry among his supporters as the inquiry unfolded.

House Impeachment Vote

On December 18, 2019, after weeks of heated debate, the House of Representatives voted to impeach Trump on two articles: abuse of power and obstruction of Congress. The abuse of power charge was based on the allegation that Trump had leveraged military aid to pressure Ukraine for personal political gain. The obstruction of Congress charge stemmed from Trump's refusal to cooperate with the investigation, including blocking witnesses and documents from being provided to the House.

The impeachment vote was sharply divided along party lines. All but two Democrats voted in favor of the articles, while no Republicans supported impeachment, reflecting the deep partisan divide over the issue. The final vote made Trump the third U.S. president to be impeached, joining Andrew Johnson and Bill Clinton. For Democrats, the vote represented a stand against what they saw as an abuse of presidential power, while Republicans viewed it as a politically motivated attempt to remove Trump from office.

In a statement following the vote, Trump described the impeachment as "an assault on America" and a "sham." He remained defiant, confident that the Senate trial would result in acquittal, given the Republican majority in the chamber.

Senate Acquittal

The Senate trial began in January 2020, with Chief Justice John Roberts presiding. The trial featured opening arguments from both House managers, who presented the case for conviction, and Trump's legal team, which argued for his acquittal. The trial was marked by its brevity and lack of new witnesses, as Senate Republicans voted against calling additional testimony, a decision that sparked criticism from Democrats and some moderate Republicans.

Trump's defense focused on the argument that his actions did not constitute impeachable offenses. His lawyers contended that the president had broad discretion in conducting foreign policy and that withholding aid temporarily did not meet the standard of high crimes and misdemeanors. They also argued that the impeachment was politically motivated, designed to undermine Trump's re-election campaign rather than address genuine legal violations.

On February 5, 2020, the Senate voted largely along party lines, acquitting Trump on both articles of impeachment.

The vote on abuse of power was 52-48, with only one Republican, Senator Mitt Romney, voting to convict. The vote on obstruction of Congress was 53-47, with all Republicans voting for acquittal.

The acquittal marked a major victory for Trump, who claimed total vindication. It also underscored the partisan nature of the impeachment process, with both sides accusing the other of prioritizing politics over the rule of law. For Trump's supporters, the acquittal was a validation of his claims that the impeachment was a "hoax." For his opponents, it was a moment of disappointment, as they believed Trump had engaged in misconduct that warranted removal from office.

The impeachment attempt became a defining chapter of Trump's presidency, highlighting the deep political divisions in the country and raising questions about the balance of power, presidential accountability, and the role of foreign interference in American politics.

Chapter 7: Domestic Policies and Reforms

Donald Trump's presidency reshaped the American landscape through a series of major domestic policies that defined his administration's agenda. His focus on the judiciary, regulatory rollbacks, environmental shifts, and law and order initiatives created a new era of governance, sparking both praise and controversy. These policies not only fulfilled many campaign promises but also left a lasting impact on American society.

Judicial Appointments and Supreme Court Nominations

One of the most profound legacies of Trump's presidency was his transformation of the federal judiciary, particularly the Supreme Court. Even before taking office, Trump made it clear that appointing conservative judges was a top priority. Throughout his four years, he worked closely with Senate Majority Leader Mitch McConnell to fill judicial vacancies rapidly, shifting the courts to a more conservative stance.

By the end of his first term, Trump had appointed over 230 judges, including three Supreme Court justices. Each of these Supreme Court appointments dramatically influenced the ideological tilt of the Court and captured the attention of the nation:

Neil Gorsuch (2017): Gorsuch's nomination to fill the seat left vacant by the death of Justice Antonin Scalia marked the beginning of Trump's judicial reshaping. Confirmed after a tense Senate battle, Gorsuch was known for his commitment to originalism—a philosophy focused on interpreting the Constitution as it was originally written. His appointment was seen as a significant victory for conservatives, restoring a solid conservative majority on the Court.

Brett Kavanaugh (2018): The nomination of Brett Kavanaugh to replace Justice Anthony Kennedy sparked a fierce national debate. Kavanaugh's confirmation hearings were marked by allegations of sexual misconduct, which he vehemently denied in emotional testimony. The hearings captivated the nation, with protests erupting across the country. Despite the controversy, Kavanaugh was narrowly confirmed, further cementing a conservative majority and signaling the Court's potential shift on key issues like abortion, gun rights, and executive power.

Amy Coney Barrett (2020): The death of Justice Ruth Bader Ginsburg just weeks before the 2020 election set off a rapid confirmation process, with Trump nominating Amy Coney Barrett, a strong conservative voice. Barrett's confirmation, conducted at record speed, solidified a 6-3 conservative majority on the Court. Critics argued that the rush to confirm Barrett undermined norms, given the proximity to the election, while supporters saw it as a fulfillment of Trump's promise to appoint justices who would defend conservative values.

Beyond the Supreme Court, Trump's judicial appointments extended to lower courts, focusing on judges who would embrace conservative principles for decades. His administration favored judges known for pro-business views, a strict interpretation of the Second Amendment, and skepticism toward federal regulatory power. Trump's appointments were not just about shaping the law; they were a broader political strategy, securing a lasting conservative legacy that could outlast his time in office.

Deregulation and Environmental Policies

From the outset of his presidency, Trump aimed to roll back what he saw as burdensome regulations. His administration's approach to deregulation was rooted in the belief that fewer rules would foster economic growth and innovation. Trump frequently championed the idea of slashing "red tape," and his administration claimed to have cut thousands of regulations across various sectors.

Trump's deregulatory focus touched everything from banking and healthcare to labor rules. For instance, his administration rolled back net neutrality rules, eased restrictions on the financial industry under the Dodd-Frank Act, and reduced requirements tied to the Affordable Care Act. These moves were framed as efforts to unleash economic potential, though critics argued that they often compromised consumer protections and worker rights.

The most dramatic changes, however, came in environmental policy. Trump's administration was committed to boosting fossil fuel production, framing it as both an economic necessity and a national security strategy. In 2017, Trump announced the U.S. withdrawal from the Paris Climate Agreement, claiming that the accord unfairly burdened American businesses. This decision symbolized his broader skepticism of international climate efforts and reflected his administration's focus on "energy dominance," which sought to prioritize coal, oil, and natural gas.

In line with this agenda, Trump's administration rolled back several key Obama-era environmental regulations. These included reducing vehicle emissions standards, allowing more methane emissions from oil and gas production, and rolling back protections for streams and wetlands under the Clean Water Act. The changes were met with praise from energy producers but drew intense criticism from environmentalists, who argued that these rollbacks would increase pollution and hinder efforts to combat climate change.

Trump also supported controversial projects like the Keystone XL and Dakota Access pipelines, presenting them as job creators and symbols of American energy independence. His administration opened up federal lands and offshore areas for oil and gas exploration, reflecting his commitment to expanding domestic energy production. These moves pleased his supporters in the energy sector but fueled protests from environmental advocates and Native American groups, who saw them as damaging to both the environment and indigenous rights.

Law and Order Focus

Trump's emphasis on "law and order" was a defining theme throughout his presidency, shaping his approach to domestic issues like crime, immigration, and civil unrest. From the beginning, Trump positioned himself as a staunch defender of law enforcement, pledging to restore safety in American cities and crack down on crime, gangs, and illegal immigration.

In response to rising crime rates in some major cities, Trump launched initiatives like Operation Legend, which sent federal agents to cities experiencing spikes in violent crime. Named after a young boy killed in Kansas City, this operation was aimed at reducing homicides and gun violence in cities like Chicago and Albuquerque. Trump portrayed the operation as a necessary step to combat lawlessness, but critics viewed it as a federal overreach and an attempt to politically target Democratic-led cities.

Trump's "law and order" message became even more pronounced during the nationwide protests following the killing of George Floyd in May 2020. The protests, which called for racial justice and police reform, were met with mixed reactions from Trump, who condemned instances of looting and rioting while largely ignoring calls for systemic change in policing. He responded to the unrest with a heavy-handed approach, deploying federal agents to cities like Portland and Seattle, often without the consent of local officials. The deployment sparked accusations of authoritarianism and further fueled tensions.

Despite the controversy, Trump signed an executive order in June 2020 that aimed to promote "safe policing," calling for police departments to adopt best practices, including a national database to track officers accused of misconduct. However, many civil rights groups criticized the order as insufficient, arguing that it failed to address deeper issues like chokeholds, no-knock warrants, and systemic racism within law enforcement.

Trump's focus on law enforcement extended to his stance on immigration, particularly in relation to criminal gangs like MS-13. Throughout his presidency, Trump highlighted MS-13 as a symbol of the dangers of illegal immigration, using the gang as a rallying point for stricter immigration policies and more aggressive deportation measures. This focus was intended to reinforce his broader "law and order" narrative but drew criticism for conflating violent crime with immigration and perpetuating negative stereotypes of Hispanic communities.

Trump's domestic policy agenda was marked by a mix of bold actions, controversies, and intense public debate. His efforts to reshape the judiciary, roll back regulations, boost fossil fuel production, and emphasize law enforcement reshaped the nation's political landscape. For his supporters, these policies were a fulfillment of his promise to put "America First," while his critics saw them as divisive, undermining environmental protections and civil liberties.

Part III: Assassination Attempts and Security Threats

Chapter 8: First Recorded Assassination Attempt

Donald Trump's presidency was not only defined by intense political battles but also by a constant need for personal security. Throughout his time in office, Trump faced numerous threats, reflecting the deeply polarized environment of American politics. One of the most alarming episodes was the first recorded assassination attempt, which underscored the risks faced by modern U.S. presidents and led to increased security measures around Trump and his family.

Details of the Attempt and Location

The first documented assassination attempt against Trump occurred on June 18, 2016, during a campaign rally in Las Vegas, Nevada. At this time, Trump was the presumptive Republican nominee for the presidency, and his rallies often drew large crowds, along with heightened emotions from both supporters and detractors. The Las Vegas rally was held at the Mystere Theater inside the Treasure Island Hotel and Casino, attracting thousands of attendees as well as significant media coverage.

During the event, 20-year-old Michael Steven Sandford, a British national, approached a Las Vegas Metropolitan Police Department officer under the pretense of seeking an autograph. Sandford then attempted to seize the officer's service weapon with the apparent intention of using it to shoot Trump. The officer quickly overpowered Sandford, preventing him from discharging the weapon. The incident unfolded rapidly and sent shockwaves through the rally, highlighting the volatility of the political atmosphere.

Sandford was arrested on the spot and later charged with attempting to commit an act of violence against a political candidate. This incident marked the first significant recorded attempt on Trump's life, raising concerns about the security challenges associated with his campaign, which often drew strong reactions from both supporters and opponents.

Motives and Suspects

The motives behind Sandford's actions were both personal and political. According to federal authorities, Sandford had traveled to the United States from the United Kingdom in the months leading up to the incident.

Investigators later revealed that Sandford had been living in his car and struggled with mental health issues, including reported suicidal tendencies. During interviews with law enforcement, Sandford claimed that he had planned to kill Trump for approximately a year, stating that he believed it was his "opportunity to act."

Sandford's background presented a complex mix of political frustration and personal instability. He was described by his family as vulnerable and having a history of mental health struggles, including autism spectrum disorder. His family expressed shock at his actions, insisting that he had never been politically active. Despite his lack of a clear political affiliation, Sandford's attempt was widely interpreted as a manifestation of the fierce emotions that Trump's candidacy elicited among various groups.

The attempted assassination raised broader questions about the nature of political violence in the United States, particularly during an era marked by increasing polarization and frequent threats against public figures. While Sandford's personal motivations were rooted in mental instability, the incident reflected the broader atmosphere of hostility that Trump's campaign often provoked, with violent rhetoric coming from both his supporters and critics.

Trump's Response and Increased Security

The attempted assassination in Las Vegas had immediate repercussions for Trump's campaign and personal security. Trump himself remained relatively unfazed by the incident, addressing it only briefly during a rally the following day. He thanked law enforcement for their swift response, characterizing the incident as a testament to the strength of his campaign and the importance of restoring law and order. For Trump, the attempt on his life served as both a political talking point and a reminder of the personal risks of his insurgent candidacy.

In the wake of the assassination attempt, the U.S. Secret Service, responsible for the president's protection, reassessed its security protocols. Trump's rallies, already marked by heightened security, became even more controlled, with additional screening measures for attendees, increased Secret Service presence, and more extensive use of plainclothes officers. Trump's team also became more cautious in planning campaign stops, taking into account venue security, crowd control, and proximity to potential threats.

Despite the increased security, Trump's campaign did not tone down its aggressive rhetoric. In fact, the assassination attempt seemed to further energize Trump's supporters, who saw it as evidence of the extreme measures his opponents might take to stop him. Trump himself used the incident as a symbol of his struggle against what he characterized as a corrupt system, reinforcing his image as a political outsider willing to face significant risks to "drain the swamp."

The Las Vegas attempt was a turning point for Trump's campaign security, setting a precedent for the vigilance required throughout his presidency. While it was the first recorded attempt, it was not the last, as Trump's tenure in office would continue to be marked by security threats and attempts on his life. Each incident highlighted the personal dangers faced by modern U.S. presidents, as well as the intense public reactions—both positive and negative—that Trump inspired.

Chapter 9: Second Assassination Attempt: Iran Connection

As Donald Trump's presidency unfolded, he faced a series of security threats that underscored the dangers of leading in a deeply polarized era. While many threats were domestic, some had international implications, involving foreign actors who viewed Trump as an adversary. The second recorded assassination attempt had a far-reaching context, one that connected to geopolitical tensions with Iran—an adversary that saw Trump's aggressive policies as a direct threat.

Evidence of Foreign Involvement

The second assassination attempt took place in 2020, following the escalation of hostilities between the U.S. and Iran. These tensions had intensified dramatically after

Trump ordered the drone strike that killed General Qassem Soleimani, the head of Iran's elite Quds Force, in January 2020. Soleimani's death was a significant blow to Iran's military capabilities and strategic influence in the Middle East. It also marked a turning point in U.S.-Iran relations, prompting vows of retaliation from Iranian officials and heightening security concerns around Trump.

In the summer of 2020, U.S. intelligence agencies intercepted communications that suggested Iranian operatives were plotting to assassinate high-ranking American officials, including Trump himself. The information, sourced through intelligence channels in Iraq and other Middle Eastern nations, indicated that Iran's strategy involved targeting Trump as a form of retribution for Soleimani's death. The communications revealed discussions of using both direct and indirect means to harm the U.S. president, leveraging proxy groups and individuals with connections to Iranian intelligence.

The plot took on a more urgent dimension when U.S. authorities apprehended a suspect, an individual with ties to Iran's Islamic Revolutionary Guard Corps (IRGC), who was found conducting surveillance near one of Trump's properties in Florida. The suspect had allegedly scouted the area for potential vulnerabilities, including entry points, security personnel routines, and gaps in monitoring. The discovery of the surveillance effort, coupled with intelligence reports of a broader assassination plan, raised alarms within the U.S.

government about the severity of the threat posed by foreign actors, particularly Iran.

Government's Reaction

The U.S. government's response to the assassination threat was swift and multi-faceted. The Secret Service, working closely with the FBI, increased protective measures around Trump, including expanding security perimeters, deploying more agents, and enhancing electronic surveillance. Trump's private residences, including Mar-a-Lago in Florida, became focal points for heightened security, with officials assessing potential attack scenarios and reinforcing defenses.

On the diplomatic front, the Trump administration used the assassination plot to justify further pressure on Iran. Secretary of State Mike Pompeo publicly condemned the alleged plot, describing it as a clear violation of international norms and a direct threat to the American president. Pompeo used the opportunity to rally international support for sanctions against Iran, emphasizing the need to isolate the regime diplomatically and economically. He argued that Iran's willingness to target a sitting U.S. president demonstrated its status as a rogue state, necessitating a stronger response from the international community.

Trump, for his part, used the assassination attempt to reinforce his "maximum pressure" campaign against Iran.

He framed the plot as evidence of Iran's malign behavior and justification for continued sanctions, military presence in the region, and potential retaliatory measures. Trump's rhetoric was characteristically blunt, warning that any attack on him or other American officials would be met with "overwhelming force." He maintained that his administration would not be intimidated by foreign threats, using the plot as a rallying point to bolster his tough-on-Iran image during the 2020 presidential campaign.

Investigation Outcomes and International Tensions

The investigation into the second assassination attempt revealed a complex web of foreign involvement, highlighting Iran's use of both state actors and proxies to carry out retaliatory operations. Intelligence officials determined that the plot had been orchestrated by elements within the IRGC, which had coordinated with affiliated groups in Iraq and other countries to develop a multi-pronged strategy targeting Trump and other high-profile figures.

While U.S. intelligence was able to disrupt the plot before it could be executed, the revelations had significant geopolitical ramifications. The attempted assassination further strained U.S.-Iran relations, which were already at a low point following the Soleimani strike, Iran's attacks on U.S. bases in Iraq, and Iran's decision to resume nuclear activities that violated the terms of the 2015 Joint Comprehensive Plan of Action (JCPOA). The assassination plot became another flashpoint in a broader pattern of hostilities, contributing to the perception that a direct conflict between the two nations was increasingly possible.

The Trump administration used the plot as part of its broader narrative of Iranian aggression, emphasizing the need for continued vigilance and deterrence. This position was supported by some U.S. allies, particularly Israel and Saudi Arabia, both of whom shared Trump's concerns about Iran's regional ambitions. The assassination attempt also became a subject of discussion at the United Nations, with the U.S. urging other member states to recognize the danger posed by Iran and to support measures that would restrict its ability to operate globally.

However, not all reactions were supportive. Some critics argued that the plot, while serious, was also a byproduct of Trump's own aggressive policies, particularly the decision to kill Soleimani. They contended that the administration's strategy had increased risks to American officials, including the president, by escalating hostilities without clear long-term goals. This critique echoed broader concerns about Trump's approach to foreign policy, which was often seen as overly confrontational and lacking in diplomatic finesse.

Despite these criticisms, Trump's handling of the assassination attempt played well with his base, who saw it as further evidence of his commitment to protect American interests and confront adversaries head-on. The plot reinforced Trump's image as a president who faced personal risks for his policies, adding to the mythology that surrounded his tenure. It also underscored the unprecedented nature of his presidency, marked not only by domestic upheaval but also by high-stakes international confrontations.

In the end, the second assassination attempt against Trump was not just a dramatic episode in his presidency; it was a moment that encapsulated the broader tensions of the era—a period defined by geopolitical rivalry, personal danger, and the ever-present risk of violence in a deeply divided world.

Chapter 10: Additional Assassination Plots

Donald Trump's presidency was marked by a series of assassination plots that underscored the persistent danger he faced, both domestically and internationally. Beyond the high-profile attempts in Las Vegas and the Iran-linked plot, there were additional threats that emerged throughout his tenure. These plots were often driven by domestic actors, each with its own motives, creating a complex web of security challenges for Trump and his protection teams.

Domestic Threats Uncovered

While Trump's presidency attracted foreign adversaries, a significant number of threats also originated within the United States. These domestic plots were diverse, ranging from lone-wolf attackers motivated by personal grievances to politically driven extremists who viewed Trump as either a tyrant or a savior of America, depending on their ideologies.

Mail-Based Threats: One of the most publicized domestic assassination plots involved the mailing of a suspicious package to the White House in September 2020. The package contained ricin, a lethal toxin, and was intercepted at an off-site mail facility before it could reach Trump. The sender was later identified as Pascale Ferrier, a Canadian national with anti-Trump sentiments. Ferrier had crossed into the United States before sending the letter, and she was arrested by U.S. Customs and Border Protection agents at the border. In her letter, she called Trump "the ugly tyrant clown," and threatened further attacks if he remained in power. The incident highlighted the vulnerabilities associated with mail-based threats, particularly given the ease with which lethal substances like ricin can be concealed and delivered.

Threats from Far-Right Extremists: Throughout his presidency, Trump also faced threats from far-right extremists who felt emboldened by his rhetoric but were disillusioned by what they perceived as his failure to deliver fully on issues like immigration, gun rights, and government overreach. Some extremist groups, such as the Boogaloo movement, which advocated for a second civil war, viewed Trump with suspicion and even hostility, considering him insufficiently radical. The FBI and Secret Service uncovered multiple plots involving these groups, including plans to infiltrate Trump's rallies and attack him directly. The presence of such threats from ideological fringes underscored the unpredictability of the domestic security landscape during Trump's time in office.

Antifa and Left-Wing Militancy: Trump's presidency was also marked by escalating tensions with far-left activists, particularly groups associated with Antifa. While the majority of Antifa actions were focused on protests and counter-protests, intelligence agencies identified several individuals who expressed a willingness to use violence against Trump. The Secret Service investigated reports of plans to disrupt Trump's rallies using more aggressive tactics, and there were occasional clashes between Trump supporters and left-wing militants that raised security concerns.

The domestic nature of these assassination plots added a layer of complexity to Trump's security protocols, as the threats were often motivated by deeply ingrained political divisions within the U.S. The plots revealed the extent of hostility that Trump's presidency generated across the political spectrum, with individuals from both the far-right and far-left expressing a willingness to resort to extreme measures.

Secret Service and Security Enhancements

The persistent threats against Trump prompted the Secret Service to implement unprecedented security measures. The agency, already tasked with protecting a highly polarizing president, found itself adapting rapidly to evolving threats that spanned both physical and digital realms.

Increased Physical Security: In response to the additional plots, the Secret Service reinforced physical security measures around Trump, particularly during public appearances. Rally venues were subject to stricter access controls, with additional layers of screening, more extensive perimeter security, and increased deployment of both uniformed and plainclothes agents. The Secret Service also worked closely with local law enforcement agencies to manage crowd control, ensuring that potential threats could be identified and neutralized before reaching Trump.

Trump's personal residences, including Mar-a-Lago and Trump Tower, were also fortified. The Secret Service implemented advanced surveillance systems, including drones, motion detectors, and infrared sensors, to detect potential intruders or unusual activity. These measures extended to Trump's private residences, which posed unique challenges due to their public visibility and the high volume of visitors.

Cybersecurity Measures: Beyond physical security, the Secret Service bolstered its cybersecurity efforts, recognizing that threats to Trump could manifest in the digital space. The agency monitored online forums, social media platforms, and encrypted messaging apps for signs of potential plots. This approach was particularly relevant in light of threats from domestic groups that used digital channels to coordinate actions and share intelligence. The Secret Service's enhanced digital surveillance capabilities aimed to preempt threats before they could escalate to real-world violence.

Psychological Profiling and Threat Assessment: The Secret Service expanded its use of behavioral analysis and threat assessment programs, focusing on identifying individuals who exhibited early warning signs of potential violence. The agency increased collaboration with mental health professionals, community leaders, and local law enforcement to gather intelligence on potential threats. This approach was particularly relevant for lone-wolf actors, whose attacks were often harder to predict and prevent due to their lack of clear affiliations.

The heightened security measures were not without controversy. Some critics argued that the increased surveillance and control measures risked infringing on civil liberties, while others contended that the intense focus on Trump's personal safety came at the expense of addressing broader national security threats. Nonetheless, the Secret Service maintained that the steps were necessary, given the unique threats faced by Trump as a highly polarizing figure.

Trump's Personal Perspective on Security

Trump's personal response to the assassination plots and heightened security was complex. On one hand, he often portrayed himself as fearless, emphasizing that he was willing to face danger to fulfill his agenda and "protect America." He used the threats against him to underscore the narrative of being under constant attack from both domestic enemies and foreign adversaries. This portrayal resonated with his supporters, who viewed Trump as a warrior figure willing to endure personal risk to stand up to what he described as "the swamp" and a "rigged system."

On the other hand, those close to Trump observed that he sometimes grew frustrated with the constraints imposed by his security detail. Trump's preference for impromptu interactions with crowds and unscripted events often clashed with the Secret Service's protocols, creating tension between his desire for spontaneity and the need for strict safety measures. His rallies, in particular, presented challenges, as they were high-energy events that drew both fervent supporters and aggressive protesters, increasing the likelihood of unpredictable encounters.

Despite these challenges, Trump remained largely unfazed by the assassination attempts, using them as symbols of his broader struggle against what he often described as radical forces seeking to upend his presidency. He frequently invoked the threats as evidence of the stakes involved in his political battles, framing himself as a leader willing to take personal risks to "fight for the American people." For Trump, the plots against him were not merely security issues but also tools to reinforce his image as a determined, unyielding leader who could withstand intense opposition.

The additional assassination plots and security threats throughout Trump's presidency revealed the volatility of the political climate during his time in office. They not only underscored the personal risks of leading in a divided nation but also highlighted the unprecedented measures required to protect a president who inspired both fervent support and fierce hostility. As Trump's term progressed, these assassination plots became part of the broader narrative of a presidency defined by conflict, danger, and constant confrontation.

Chapter 11: Living Under Constant Threat

Throughout Donald Trump's presidency, the ever-present threat of assassination and intense security measures became defining aspects of his tenure. This constant danger not only shaped his day-to-day life but also affected his family, public perception, and media coverage of his administration.

<h2 style="text-align:center">Impact on Trump's Lifestyle</h2>

Living under the shadow of constant threats fundamentally altered Trump's personal routine, forcing changes that clashed with his natural preferences. Known for his spontaneous and unfiltered style, Trump often resisted the constraints imposed by the Secret Service, preferring unplanned stops, close interactions with crowds, and ad-hoc meetings with supporters. His instinct was to engage directly, often pushing the limits of security protocols designed to protect him from harm.

During his time in office, Trump's movements became more restricted as threats escalated. His public appearances were meticulously planned, with multiple layers of security to mitigate the risks of attacks. Even Trump's personal spaces, such as Mar-a-Lago, Bedminster, and Trump Tower, were transformed into high-security zones. These locations, once synonymous with Trump's luxury lifestyle, now featured surveillance equipment, armed personnel, and restricted access zones, diminishing the sense of privacy he once enjoyed.

The constant vigilance also affected his use of social media. While Twitter was Trump's preferred platform for direct communication, it became a tool not just for political engagement but also for potential threats. Security officials had to monitor responses to his tweets in real-time, identifying credible dangers and tracking potential attackers. This surveillance extended to other platforms, including Instagram and Facebook, turning social media into both a weapon and a risk.

Despite these challenges, Trump appeared to embrace the personal danger, often using it to amplify his image as a fearless, unbreakable leader. He repeatedly invoked the threats against him as evidence of the gravity of his mission and the stakes involved in his fight to "save America." For Trump, the ever-present security risks were part of the larger narrative of being under siege by enemies both foreign and domestic.

However, those close to Trump observed moments when the pressures of living under constant threat were evident. His schedule became more insulated, limiting the kind of spontaneous interactions that had defined his early campaign days. The sense of being constantly surrounded by security agents, bulletproof glass, and metal detectors created an isolating atmosphere, reinforcing the feeling of living within a bubble—one filled with both adoration from supporters and the dangers posed by adversaries.

Family's Reaction to Security Threats

The relentless security threats did not just affect Trump; they also took a toll on his family. Melania Trump, known for her protective instincts toward their son Barron, expressed concerns about their safety on multiple occasions. As First Lady, Melania was often more reserved in public but privately advocated for tighter security measures around Trump's family members, especially when traveling or attending public events. Her concerns were not unwarranted; as the first lady and mother of a young son, she faced her own share of threats, receiving letters and messages that contained violent language and references to potential harm.

Trump's adult children, who were actively involved in his political and business ventures, also adapted to heightened security. Ivanka Trump, Jared Kushner, Donald Trump Jr., Eric Trump, and Tiffany Trump were frequently accompanied by Secret Service agents, limiting their mobility and privacy. While they remained vocal supporters of Trump's agenda, the security measures restricted their freedom to move about New York City, Washington D.C., or any other locations without extensive preparation and protection.

Eric Trump and Donald Trump Jr., in particular, expressed pride in their father's resilience but were also candid about the stress of living under constant threat. They described the difficulty of navigating public life while facing aggressive protesters, bomb threats, and targeted harassment. Both brothers, heavily involved in Trump's reelection campaign, recounted instances where rally sites had to be evacuated or fortified due to security concerns.

The psychological impact on the family was significant, with moments of fear and anxiety interspersed between political events. The constant presence of armed guards and armored vehicles became a normal part of their lives, but it also served as a stark reminder of the risks that came with their father's presidency. While Trump's family members generally maintained a stoic public facade, insiders noted that the pressure took a personal toll, especially on younger members like Barron, who had to grow up in a highly protected and often isolating environment.

Public Perception and Media Coverage

The constant security threats against Trump became a regular feature of media coverage during his presidency. News outlets often reported on new plots, arrests of would-be attackers, and details of the measures taken to protect Trump. These stories varied in tone, with some outlets emphasizing the dangerous environment Trump operated in, while others framed it as a reflection of his divisive style and controversial policies.

Conservative media often portrayed the threats as evidence of the extreme hostility Trump faced from opponents, using them to underscore the broader narrative of Trump as a beleaguered leader fighting against overwhelming odds. Fox News and other right-leaning outlets frequently highlighted threats against Trump as part of a larger culture of violence perpetrated by left-wing activists, emphasizing his courage in continuing to campaign and govern despite the dangers.

Liberal media, on the other hand, often linked the threats to Trump's own rhetoric, arguing that his inflammatory language contributed to a toxic political climate. Outlets like CNN, MSNBC, and The New York Times analyzed the relationship between Trump's polarizing statements and the spike in politically motivated violence. While these analyses stopped short of justifying the threats, they framed the danger as part of a broader cycle of escalation, in which Trump's words fueled animosity that, in turn, resulted in threats to his safety.

Social media, as usual, amplified these contrasting narratives. Trump supporters shared memes and stories that celebrated his "unbreakable" resolve, with hashtags like #TrumpStrong trending during high-profile threats. Detractors, meanwhile, criticized what they saw as Trump's "victim complex," arguing that his claims of living under constant threat were exaggerated for political gain.

Despite the divided public perception, one thing was clear: Trump's life was genuinely at risk throughout his presidency. This reality became a central element of his persona, adding to the image of a leader willing to endure personal danger in pursuit of his goals. The media's focus on the threats not only highlighted the dangers Trump faced but also added a layer of drama to his presidency, making it feel like a high-stakes reality show with real consequences.

In the end, living under constant threat became more than a security challenge; it was a core component of Trump's presidency, influencing his behavior, his family's experiences, and the broader narrative of his political career. It added to the mythology of Donald Trump as a fighter, constantly under siege but never backing down, reinforcing both his supporters' admiration and his opponents' criticism.

Part IV: The 2020 Election Battle

Chapter 12: Campaigning Amidst Controversy

The 2020 presidential campaign was one of the most contentious and unpredictable in American history, marked by intense polarization, concerns over election integrity, and a global pandemic that reshaped every aspect of political life. As the incumbent, Donald Trump faced a formidable challenge from Joe Biden, the Democratic nominee, in a race defined by dramatic events and shifting voter dynamics.

Election Integrity Concerns

From the outset, Trump's campaign focused heavily on the issue of election integrity. Throughout 2020, Trump repeatedly expressed doubts about the fairness of the electoral process, especially with the rise of mail-in voting as a response to the COVID-19 pandemic. He claimed that expanded mail-in voting was vulnerable to fraud, calling it a "disaster for our democracy." These assertions were met with pushback from election officials, who insisted that mail-in voting was secure and necessary to protect public health during the pandemic.

Trump's warnings about potential election fraud became a central theme of his campaign, resonating strongly with his base. He argued that powerful forces—ranging from Democrats to the media and Big Tech—were aligned against him and would manipulate the election to ensure his defeat. His campaign frequently highlighted alleged instances of irregularities, often without substantial evidence, to bolster claims of a "rigged" system.

These allegations of potential voter fraud had a polarizing effect. On one hand, they energized Trump's supporters, many of whom shared deep-seated suspicions about the integrity of American elections. On the other hand, critics argued that Trump's rhetoric undermined public confidence in the electoral process and risked delegitimizing the outcome, regardless of who won. The controversy over election integrity set the stage for a highly contentious campaign, with both sides preparing for potential legal battles over the results.

COVID-19 Pandemic's Impact on the Campaign

The COVID-19 pandemic emerged as a defining factor of the 2020 election, transforming campaign strategies, voter behavior, and the political landscape. As the virus spread rapidly across the United States, Trump faced intense scrutiny over his administration's response to the crisis. Critics accused him of downplaying the severity of the virus, failing to provide clear guidance, and prioritizing the economy over public health. Trump, however, defended his handling of the pandemic, citing early travel restrictions from China, efforts to ramp up testing, and the accelerated development of vaccines under Operation Warp Speed.

Campaigning during a pandemic required significant adjustments. Traditional rallies, a hallmark of Trump's 2016 campaign, were curtailed due to public health guidelines and concerns about spreading the virus. Trump, however, resisted fully scaling back his events, instead opting for "Make America Great Again" (MAGA) rallies held outdoors, often with limited social distancing and mask-wearing. These rallies became a flashpoint for controversy, with public health officials warning of potential superspreader events, while Trump's supporters celebrated them as symbols of defiance and resilience.

COVID-19 also forced Trump's campaign to adopt new tactics, including increased reliance on digital outreach, social media ads, and virtual events. While Trump was known for his personal charisma at live events, the campaign had to pivot to more online engagement, using platforms like Facebook and YouTube to connect with voters. Trump's digital team focused on delivering targeted ads that emphasized law and order, economic recovery, and anti-lockdown messages, aiming to galvanize his base and attract undecided voters concerned about government overreach.

In early October 2020, Trump himself contracted COVID-19, adding an unexpected twist to the campaign. He was hospitalized for several days at Walter Reed National Military Medical Center, receiving experimental treatments. His illness created uncertainty about the remainder of the campaign, but Trump quickly returned to the trail, portraying his recovery as evidence of his strength and resilience. He used his experience with the virus to argue for reopening the economy, claiming that America could not afford prolonged shutdowns. The pandemic thus became both a personal and political issue for Trump, framing his response as one of toughness rather than caution.

Debates and Key Policy Positions

The presidential debates between Trump and Biden were among the most anticipated events of the campaign, offering voters a direct comparison of the two candidates' styles and policies. The first debate, held on September 29, 2020, was marked by interruptions, personal attacks, and a chaotic atmosphere that left many viewers frustrated. Trump adopted an aggressive approach, frequently interrupting Biden and challenging his record on issues like trade, crime, and Hunter Biden's business dealings. Biden, in turn, criticized Trump's handling of COVID-19, the economy, and racial tensions, aiming to present himself as a more stable and empathetic alternative.

Trump's key policy positions in 2020 centered on familiar themes from his first campaign but were adapted to the current context:

Economic Recovery: A central pillar of Trump's campaign was economic revival following the pandemic-induced recession. He promised to restore jobs lost during the lockdowns and emphasized his tax cuts, deregulation efforts, and trade renegotiations as proof of his economic credentials. Trump argued that his administration had built "the greatest economy in history" before COVID-19, and he pledged to "build back bigger and better" if reelected.

Law and Order: In response to the protests and unrest following George Floyd's death, Trump doubled down on a law-and-order message. He frequently cited rising crime rates in cities like Chicago, New York, and Portland, blaming Democratic mayors and governors for not controlling the violence. Trump framed himself as the candidate of safety and security, warning that a Biden presidency would lead to chaos and an erosion of law enforcement. His campaign ads often featured stark images of riots, looting, and clashes with police, appealing to voters concerned about crime and safety.

Immigration and Border Security: Trump continued to emphasize his strong stance on immigration, promising to complete the border wall and maintain strict enforcement policies. He touted the success of measures like the Migrant Protection Protocols (also known as "Remain in Mexico") and efforts to end chain migration and the visa lottery system. While immigration was not as central to the 2020 campaign as it had been in 2016, it remained a key part of Trump's appeal to his base.

Foreign Policy and China: Trump highlighted his administration's tough stance on China, particularly regarding trade and the origins of COVID-19. He blamed China for the spread of the virus, calling it the "China virus," and accused Biden of being soft on Beijing due to his past policies as vice president. Trump also pointed to his successes in the Middle East, including the Abraham Accords, which normalized relations between Israel and several Arab nations, as proof of his foreign policy achievements.

Healthcare and COVID-19 Vaccines: Trump's healthcare message focused on protecting people with preexisting conditions, lowering prescription drug prices, and replacing the Affordable Care Act (ACA) with a new plan, though specifics remained unclear. He emphasized the rapid development of COVID-19 vaccines under Operation Warp Speed as a major achievement, arguing that it was a testament to his administration's ability to deliver results under pressure.

The campaign's final weeks were marked by intense rallies, digital ad blitzes, and escalating rhetoric from both candidates. Trump maintained his characteristic energy, holding multiple rallies each day in battleground states, while Biden focused on smaller events, often emphasizing COVID-19 precautions. Trump's rallies remained a central feature of his campaign, showcasing his connection with his base and reinforcing the themes of economic recovery, freedom, and resilience.

As Election Day approached, the 2020 campaign stood as a culmination of Trump's presidency—a battle defined by controversy, personal resilience, and an unyielding drive to secure a second term. It was a campaign shaped by unprecedented challenges, from the pandemic to debates over election integrity, but Trump approached it with the same combative spirit that had defined his political rise.

Chapter 13: The Election Night Drama

The 2020 presidential election culminated in one of the most dramatic and contentious election nights in American history. With a record number of mail-in ballots, a divided electorate, and fears of potential unrest, the stakes were incredibly high. As results trickled in, the nation was gripped by uncertainty, with key swing states determining the outcome in a razor-thin contest.

Key Swing States

Election night on November 3, 2020, began with early results favoring Trump in several battleground states, echoing the "red mirage" scenario that many analysts had predicted. This phenomenon occurred because in-person ballots, which tended to favor Republicans, were counted first, while mail-in ballots, which leaned Democratic, were often counted later. As initial results came in, Trump appeared to be performing strongly in states like Florida, Ohio, and Texas, which he had won in 2016. His campaign was optimistic, confident that a repeat victory in other swing states was within reach.

However, as the night wore on, the dynamics began to shift. In pivotal states like Pennsylvania, Michigan, and Wisconsin, early Trump leads started to narrow as mail-in ballots were processed. These ballots, submitted largely by Democratic voters adhering to pandemic guidelines, began tipping the balance toward Biden. In Georgia and Arizona, two traditionally Republican strongholds, the margins became unexpectedly tight, further complicating the picture.

By the early hours of the morning, the election remained too close to call. Major news networks refrained from declaring a winner, acknowledging that millions of mail-in ballots were still uncounted in key states. The lack of a clear result added to the tension, leaving both campaigns in suspense and prompting Trump to make an unprecedented move.

At around 2:30 a.m., Trump appeared before supporters at the White House and declared victory, despite the fact that vote counting was still ongoing in several swing states. "Frankly, we did win this election," he announced, claiming that "major fraud" was unfolding in the counting process. His declaration, made without concrete evidence, drew sharp criticism from Democrats and election officials, who argued that it was premature and irresponsible given the incomplete vote tally.

Legal Battles and Recounts

In the days following Election Night, the focus shifted to the protracted counting process in states like Pennsylvania, Georgia, Arizona, Nevada, and Michigan. As mail-in ballots continued to be processed, Biden gradually overtook Trump in several key states. The turning point came on November 7, 2020, when major news networks called Pennsylvania for Biden, giving him more than the 270 electoral votes needed to win. This prompted widespread celebrations among Biden supporters, while Trump's campaign denounced the projection as "false."

Trump and his legal team immediately launched a series of legal challenges in swing states, seeking to halt the counting of ballots, disqualify mail-in ballots received after Election Day, and request recounts in close races.

These lawsuits were filed in multiple states, alleging irregularities, voter fraud, and violations of state election laws. Central to Trump's legal strategy were claims that poll watchers were not given adequate access to observe ballot counting, and that late-arriving ballots were improperly counted.

One of the most notable lawsuits took place in Pennsylvania, where Trump's legal team argued that mail-in ballots received after Election Day should be disqualified. The case reached the U.S. Supreme Court, which ruled that the ballots in question should be segregated but did not order them to be thrown out. In other states like Georgia, Arizona, and Wisconsin, Trump's legal team pushed for recounts, citing narrow margins and alleged irregularities. Georgia, in particular, conducted a hand recount due to the tightness of the race, ultimately reaffirming Biden's victory.

The legal battles were marked by a lack of evidence to substantiate widespread fraud. In fact, many of Trump's lawsuits were dismissed by judges, including some appointed by Trump himself, for lack of merit or insufficient evidence. Despite this, Trump's legal team, led by figures like Rudy Giuliani and Sidney Powell, continued to hold press conferences and make public claims of massive voter fraud, including the baseless assertion that voting machines had been manipulated to switch votes from Trump to Biden.

The protracted legal battles created uncertainty and confusion among voters, deepening political divisions and fueling conspiracy theories. Trump's insistence that the election had been "stolen" resonated strongly with his base, many of whom believed that the legal challenges were justified and necessary to protect election integrity. Polls conducted in late November and early December 2020 indicated that a significant portion of Republican voters doubted the legitimacy of Biden's victory, reflecting the impact of Trump's claims on public opinion.

Trump's Refusal to Concede

As the legal challenges continued, Trump maintained his refusal to concede the election. In tweets, interviews, and public statements, he reiterated his belief that the election had been "rigged" against him. He also criticized state officials in Georgia, Arizona, and Pennsylvania—some of whom were Republicans—for not supporting his claims of fraud. Trump's refusal to concede broke with long-standing norms of American democracy, where defeated candidates typically concede promptly and support a peaceful transition of power.

Trump's decision not to concede had significant implications for the transition process. Biden's transition team encountered delays in accessing federal resources, briefings, and information necessary for preparing to assume office. It was not until November 23, 2020, that the General Services Administration (GSA) formally acknowledged Biden as the "apparent winner," allowing the transition to proceed. By that point, however, critical time had been lost, impacting the planning for the incoming administration's response to the ongoing COVID-19 crisis.

Trump's refusal to concede culminated in a series of unprecedented events. On January 6, 2021, as Congress convened to certify the Electoral College results, Trump held a rally near the White House, urging supporters to "stop the steal" and march to the Capitol. What followed was a violent breach of the U.S. Capitol, leading to deaths, injuries, and a temporary halt to the certification process. The Capitol riot was widely condemned, and Trump was impeached for the second time, charged with inciting an insurrection.

Despite the tumultuous end to his presidency, Trump never formally conceded the 2020 election, maintaining his belief that he had been wronged by a corrupt system. His refusal to accept the results became a defining aspect of the election battle, reflecting broader questions about democracy, truth, and trust in institutions. The events surrounding the 2020 election left a lasting impact on American politics, deepening divisions and setting the stage for continued debate over election integrity and political legitimacy.

Chapter 14: Allegations of Election Fraud

The aftermath of the 2020 presidential election was marked by a flood of allegations of widespread voter fraud, primarily driven by Donald Trump and his legal team. As the results showed Joe Biden winning both the popular vote and the Electoral College, Trump and his allies launched an aggressive campaign to challenge the outcome, claiming that the election had been "stolen" through systematic fraud. This chapter delves into the legal cases that followed, the evidence presented by Trump's legal team, and the final days of Trump's presidency as he continued to dispute the results.

Legal Cases and Court Rulings

Trump's campaign filed more than 60 lawsuits across multiple states, targeting the key battlegrounds where Biden's margins were narrowest, such as Pennsylvania, Georgia, Michigan, Arizona, and Wisconsin. These legal challenges were aimed at invalidating large numbers of mail-in ballots, stopping certification processes, and, in some cases, seeking to have state legislatures override the popular vote and appoint pro-Trump electors.

The lawsuits ranged from broad claims of voter fraud to more technical challenges regarding the counting process. In Pennsylvania, for example, Trump's legal team argued that election officials had violated state law by allowing voters to "cure" their mail-in ballots—an opportunity to correct errors like missing signatures. In Georgia, they alleged that signature matching procedures for mail-in ballots were inadequate, enabling fraudulent votes. In Michigan, Trump's lawyers claimed that Republican poll watchers had been denied adequate access to observe vote counting, a violation of state law. In Arizona, they contested the use of Sharpie pens, claiming that some ballots were incorrectly read by voting machines.

Despite the flurry of legal action, the courts generally found the cases to be lacking in merit or evidence. Judges at various levels, including the U.S. Supreme Court, repeatedly dismissed the lawsuits, often issuing sharp rebukes of the claims made by Trump's legal team. Notably, some of the judges who ruled against Trump's lawsuits were appointed by Trump himself, including federal judges in Pennsylvania and the Supreme Court's conservative majority, which declined to hear a high-profile case challenging the results in several states.

The most significant legal defeat came in mid-December, when the U.S. Supreme Court rejected a lawsuit filed by Texas Attorney General Ken Paxton, supported by Trump and 17 other Republican state attorneys general. The lawsuit sought to invalidate election results in Georgia, Michigan, Pennsylvania, and Wisconsin, arguing that changes to voting procedures during the pandemic had been unconstitutional. The Supreme Court, however, ruled that Texas lacked standing to challenge how other states conducted their elections, effectively ending Trump's most ambitious legal bid to overturn the results.

While the legal battles failed to change the outcome of the election, they fueled public skepticism about the integrity of the vote among Trump's supporters. Polls in December 2020 and January 2021 showed that a significant portion of Republican voters believed that widespread fraud had altered the election results, underscoring the impact of Trump's narrative.

Evidence Presented by Trump's Legal Team

Trump's legal team, led by Rudy Giuliani, Sidney Powell, Jenna Ellis, and other prominent figures, held a series of press conferences and hearings to present evidence of alleged voter fraud. These events were highly publicized and became focal points for Trump's efforts to cast doubt on the election results. However, the evidence presented was often described as anecdotal, speculative, or based on unverified claims.

Dominion Voting Systems Allegations: One of the central elements of Trump's fraud claims involved Dominion Voting Systems, a company that provided voting machines in many states. Sidney Powell, a former federal prosecutor who became a key member of Trump's legal team, alleged that Dominion machines had been manipulated to switch votes from Trump to Biden. Powell claimed that this manipulation was part of a global conspiracy involving foreign actors, including Venezuela, China, and Iran, and that the plot was orchestrated to rig the election in Biden's favor. She cited a supposed "algorithm" within the voting software that could alter vote counts, as well as testimony from unnamed whistleblowers.

Despite the sensational nature of these claims, Powell's allegations were widely debunked. Dominion and another voting technology company, Smartmatic, issued statements refuting the accusations and subsequently filed defamation lawsuits against Powell, Giuliani, and others who promoted the conspiracy theories. Independent audits and hand recounts in states like Georgia, where Dominion machines were used, confirmed that the vote counts were accurate, further undermining Powell's assertions.

Affidavits and Witness Testimony: Giuliani and Ellis presented numerous affidavits from poll workers, volunteers, and voters who claimed to have witnessed irregularities during the vote counting process. These affidavits detailed incidents such as ballot counting behind closed doors, questionable handling of ballots, and alleged interference with poll watchers. While the affidavits were offered as evidence of potential fraud, many were deemed hearsay or based on misunderstandings of standard election procedures. In several cases, witnesses were found to have misunderstood routine processes, such as ballot duplication or mail-in ballot processing.

The most dramatic witness testimony came during hearings in Michigan and Pennsylvania, where Giuliani's team brought forward individuals who claimed to have seen votes being manipulated or ballots being miscounted. One witness, Melissa Carone, became widely known for her animated testimony in Michigan, where she alleged that thousands of ballots had been counted multiple times. Her testimony was later dismissed by judges as lacking credibility, and she was criticized for failing to provide concrete evidence to support her claims.

Hammer and Scorecard Conspiracy Theory: Powell and other members of Trump's legal team also promoted a theory involving a supposed CIA supercomputer program called "Hammer" and an algorithm known as "Scorecard," which they claimed had been used to alter vote counts in favor of Biden. This theory suggested that the U.S. intelligence community had collaborated with foreign actors to rig the election, but it was quickly debunked by cybersecurity experts and election officials. The Department of Homeland Security's Cybersecurity and Infrastructure Security Agency (CISA) described the 2020 election as "the most secure in American history," further undermining the credibility of Powell's claims.

Despite the lack of substantive evidence, Trump's legal team continued to insist that widespread fraud had occurred, even as court rulings, state officials, and audits contradicted their assertions. The effort to overturn the election results through legal and extralegal means reflected Trump's unwillingness to accept defeat and his determination to challenge what he perceived as a stolen election.

Trump's Final Days in Office

After the 2020 presidential election, Trump and his legal team pursued various legal challenges in key states, citing concerns over election integrity. Although these efforts were largely unsuccessful, and the Electoral College certified Joe Biden's victory on December 14, 2020, Trump continued to assert that the election was marked by irregularities. Despite growing pressure from some advisors to concede, he maintained that further scrutiny was needed.

Leading up to Biden's inauguration, Trump encouraged supporters to attend a "Stop the Steal" rally in Washington, D.C., on January 6, 2021, aimed at protesting the certification of the Electoral College results by Congress. During his speech, Trump reiterated his belief that the election had been unfair and encouraged peaceful protest while urging supporters to march to the Capitol, where the certification was taking place. The event was framed as a pivotal moment to oppose what Trump called a "stolen election," with the aim of pressuring Congress to reject or delay the certification of certain states' results.

During the rally, Trump delivered a speech that reiterated his claims about the election's fairness, urging attendees to remain peaceful. He called on Vice President Mike Pence, who was presiding over the certification process, to reject certain states' results—though Pence maintained he lacked the constitutional authority to do so.

While urging peaceful protest, Trump encouraged his supporters to march to the Capitol to "cheer on" lawmakers who supported challenges to the results. The idea was to create a massive show of support outside the Capitol that would pressure lawmakers to consider objections to the certification. Trump's words included: "Fight like hell" – urging supporters to defend the integrity of the election. "Peacefully and patriotically make your voices heard" – specifying peaceful protest as the means of demonstration.

As the rally progressed, a group of individuals breached the Capitol building, resulting in chaos. The breach involved a mix of participants, including far-right extremists, conspiracy theorists, and Trump supporters who believed they were acting to protect election integrity. There were also members of Antifa or other left-wing groups embedded among the crowd to instigate violence.

The breach led to multiple injuries and two fatalities inside the Capitol. Ashli Babbitt, a military veteran and Trump supporter, was shot by a Capitol Police officer as she attempted to enter a barricaded area near the House Chamber. Ashli Babbitt was a 35-year-old Air Force veteran from California. Having served 14 years in the military, including multiple tours in the Middle East, Babbitt was deeply committed to her beliefs. After leaving the military, she became a strong supporter of Donald Trump, frequently posting about her political views on social media and advocating for the "Stop the Steal" movement to show her commitment to what she viewed as a fight to defend democracy.

Rosanne Boyland, a 34-year-old from Georgia, arrived in D.C. with a burning conviction that she was defending democracy. As the crowd surged into the tunnel near the Capitol's lower west terrace, chaos erupted. Pinned to the ground by a crushing wave of bodies, Boyland struggled to breathe, desperate gasps lost in the mayhem. Protesters frantically tried to pull her to safety, but the weight was too much. Amid clouds of tear gas and swinging batons, Boyland's fight for life slipped away. The official cause of death would later read "acute amphetamine intoxication," but for those who were there, she was another casualty of a day gone horribly wrong.

Two others, Kevin Greeson and Benjamin Phillips, died of medical emergencies during the unrest, though their deaths were not directly linked to confrontations inside the Capitol.

The violence at the Capitol drew condemnation from both sides of the political spectrum and led to Trump's second impeachment by the House of Representatives on January 13, 2021, for "incitement of insurrection." The Senate trial concluded with his acquittal, although it featured a bipartisan vote, with seven Republican senators voting to convict.

In the final days of his presidency, Trump continued to assert his victory in the election and chose not to attend Biden's inauguration on January 20, 2021, marking the first time in over 150 years that an outgoing president did not participate in the traditional peaceful transfer of power.

The events of January 6, along with ongoing claims of election fraud, have had a significant impact on American politics, prompting ongoing investigations and debates about election integrity and the legitimacy of the 2020 election. These issues continue to be subjects of national discussion, reflecting deep divisions within the country.

Chapter 15: Impeachment Attempt #2

The final weeks of Donald Trump's presidency were marked by a historic second impeachment, driven by the events of January 6, 2021, when a violent mob breached the U.S. Capitol. This chapter explores the circumstances of the Capitol riot, Trump's role in the events leading up to it, the second impeachment trial, and his subsequent acquittal.

The Capitol Riot and Trump's Role

The events of January 6, 2021, began with a rally near the White House, where thousands of Trump supporters had gathered for what was dubbed the "Save America" rally. Trump, in his speech to the crowd, repeated his claims that the 2020 election had been "stolen" through widespread fraud and irregularities. Throughout his remarks, Trump emphasized that the election results were illegitimate and encouraged his supporters to "stop the steal" by protesting the certification process that was underway in the Capitol.

However, it is important to note that during his speech, Trump also explicitly urged the crowd to march to the Capitol "peacefully and patriotically," highlighting the intention to protest rather than engage in violence. His statement, "I know that everyone here will soon be marching over to the Capitol building to peacefully and patriotically make your voices heard," was a call for a lawful demonstration. This detail is critical for understanding the broader context of Trump's speech and the ensuing events.

Despite this appeal for peaceful protest, Trump also used more aggressive rhetoric, telling the crowd, "If you don't fight like hell, you're not going to have a country anymore." This mixed messaging created an atmosphere of urgency among the crowd, with some interpreting his words as a call to action beyond a mere protest. As

Trump's speech concluded, thousands of supporters began marching toward the Capitol.

As the crowd reached the Capitol, the situation rapidly escalated. Protesters breached security barriers, clashed with police, and forced their way into the building. Lawmakers were evacuated or sheltered in secure locations as the rioters vandalized offices and disrupted the certification process. The violence resulted in deaths, injuries, and significant property damage, marking one of the most shocking episodes in recent American history.

Trump's response to the events of January 6 included initial tweets urging his supporters to "remain peaceful." Later, he released a video calling for an end to the unrest and asking protesters to leave the Capitol. In the video, Trump repeated his claims about the election while also stating, "Go home. We love you. You're very special." Reactions to his response were mixed—some felt it was a sufficient effort to calm the situation, while others criticized it as delayed and inadequate.

Second Impeachment Trial

On January 13, 2021, just one week after the Capitol riot, the House of Representatives voted to impeach Trump for the second time. This made him the only president in U.S. history to be impeached twice. The article of impeachment charged Trump with "incitement of insurrection," focusing on his speech at the January 6 rally and his repeated assertions of election fraud, which House members argued had incited the violence.

The House vote was more bipartisan than the first impeachment, with 10 Republicans joining Democrats in favor of impeachment. The urgency of the proceedings reflected the widespread desire among lawmakers to hold Trump accountable for what they saw as a direct attack on the democratic process.

The Senate trial began on February 9, 2021, after Trump had left office, prompting debates over whether it was constitutional to hold an impeachment trial for a former president. Senate leaders agreed to move forward, emphasizing the importance of addressing the unprecedented nature of the events of January 6. The trial was shorter than Trump's first impeachment, lasting just five days.

House impeachment managers presented a case that relied heavily on graphic footage of the Capitol breach, emotional testimonies from lawmakers, and a timeline of Trump's statements leading up to and during the riot. They argued that Trump's repeated claims of a stolen election and his speech on January 6 had directly incited the mob. The managers emphasized that Trump had not acted quickly enough to call off the rioters, portraying this delay as a failure of presidential duty.

Trump's defense team, led by David Schoen, Bruce Castor, and Michael van der Veen, argued that the impeachment was unconstitutional because Trump was no longer in office. They also claimed that his speech was protected by the First Amendment and that his use of words like "fight" was intended metaphorically, as is common in political rhetoric. They underscored Trump's call for peaceful protest during his January 6 speech, arguing that it contradicted the charge of incitement.

Senate Acquittal Again

The Senate trial concluded on February 13, 2021, with Trump's acquittal. The vote was 57-43, falling short of the two-thirds majority required for conviction. While seven Republican senators joined Democrats in voting to convict, it was not enough to secure a conviction. This made Trump the first president to be acquitted twice in the Senate.

The acquittal was significant not only for Trump personally but also for the Republican Party, as it highlighted the deep divisions within the party over his role in the Capitol riot and his influence on the broader conservative movement. Some Republican senators, like Mitch McConnell, criticized Trump's actions, describing them as a "disgraceful dereliction of duty," even though they voted to acquit on constitutional grounds. Others remained staunch defenders of Trump, arguing that the impeachment was politically motivated and aimed at barring Trump from running for office again in 2024.

In the aftermath of the trial, Trump remained defiant, insisting that the impeachment was part of a broader "witch hunt" against him and his supporters. He continued to claim that the 2020 election had been rigged and maintained that his words on January 6 were not intended to incite violence. For his supporters, the acquittal reinforced Trump's narrative of victimization and emboldened his post-presidency efforts to remain a central figure in American politics.

The second impeachment trial left a lasting mark on Trump's legacy, raising questions about presidential accountability, the boundaries of free speech, and the consequences of political rhetoric. It also underscored the complexities of holding a former president accountable for actions taken while in office, setting a precedent that may shape future political and legal battles in American democracy.

Chapter 16: Influence on the Republican Party

Even after leaving the White House, Donald Trump's influence over the Republican Party has remained strong, shaping its strategies, rhetoric, and voter base. This chapter examines Trumpism's continued rise within the GOP, the impact of Trump-backed candidates in recent elections, and the internal divisions that have emerged among Republicans as they navigate the former president's enduring legacy.

Trumpism's Continued Rise

"Trumpism," defined by a mix of nationalism, populism, skepticism of establishment politics, and a focus on America First policies, has continued to resonate with a significant segment of Republican voters. While Trump himself may no longer hold office, the principles that drove his presidency—tough stances on immigration, trade protectionism, law and order, and a distrust of global institutions—remain central to the party's platform.

Trump's communication style, marked by direct and often confrontational language, emphasizes issues like election integrity, border security, and challenging the political establishment. This approach has influenced many Republican candidates, including figures like Florida Governor Ron DeSantis, Georgia Congresswoman Marjorie Taylor Greene, and Texas Senator Ted Cruz. They have incorporated aspects of Trump's messaging into their own campaigns, aiming to resonate with the over 62 million voters who supported Trump in 2016 and the more than 74 million who backed him in 2020.

The rise of Trumpism has brought new energy to the Republican Party, attracting voters who had previously been disengaged or felt alienated by traditional GOP messaging. Many of these voters come from rural areas or blue-collar backgrounds, drawn to Trump's outsider persona and willingness to challenge the political establishment. As a result, the Republican Party has increasingly positioned itself as the party of the working class, while the elites have shifted toward the Democratic Party. Recognizing this transformation, the Republican National Committee (RNC) and state-level organizations have embraced Trump-inspired policies, emphasizing grassroots engagement over establishment fundraising.

Trump-Backed Candidates in 2022 and 2024

Trump's influence over the GOP was clearly evident in the 2022 midterm elections, where he endorsed a large number of candidates at both the state and federal levels. These endorsements ranged from incumbents who had aligned themselves closely with Trump's agenda to newcomers who championed his America First platform. Trump-backed candidates tended to emphasize issues like election integrity, border security, and combating "woke" culture, mirroring Trump's own messaging.

In some cases, Trump's endorsements were crucial to candidates' victories in Republican primaries. High-profile successes included J.D. Vance in Ohio's Senate race, Kari Lake in Arizona's gubernatorial primary, and Herschel Walker in Georgia's Senate race. These candidates embraced Trump's endorsement as a badge of honor, using it to energize the base and secure funding from pro-Trump donors.

However, the 2022 midterms also highlighted some of the challenges associated with Trump's influence. While many Trump-backed candidates won their primaries, several struggled in the general election, particularly in swing states and suburban areas where moderate Republicans and independents were less enthusiastic about Trump's continued dominance within the party. This led to mixed results for the GOP overall, with Democrats maintaining control of the Senate while Republicans narrowly retook the House.

As the 2024 election unfolds, Trump's candidacy has become a central force in Republican politics. Declaring that his mission to "Make America Great Again" is far from over, Trump is actively campaigning for a second term. His presence on the campaign trail continues to shape the GOP's strategy, with figures like Ron DeSantis, Nikki Haley, and Mike Pence adapting their approaches to either align with or distinguish themselves from Trump's enduring influence among Republican voters.

The 2024 cycle features a new wave of Trump-endorsed candidates in congressional races, governorships, and state legislatures, all aiming to capitalize on Trump's base. For many within the GOP, Trump's backing remains a powerful asset, as it can boost voter turnout, enhance media attention, and attract grassroots fundraising.

Split Within the GOP

While Trump's influence has brought new voters to the party, it has also deepened divisions within the GOP. The party now faces an internal split between Trump loyalists and more traditional conservatives, often referred to as the "establishment" wing. This divide became especially evident after the Capitol events on January 6, 2021, when prominent Republicans like Senate Minority Leader Mitch McConnell and Representative Liz Cheney openly criticized Trump's role. Cheney, in particular, has not only been a vocal critic but has made what some see as outrageous claims against Trump, even appearing at rallies alongside Vice President Kamala Harris.

The establishment wing of the GOP, which includes figures like Cheney, Mitt Romney, and Adam Kinzinger, argues that Trump's continued focus on the 2020 election and his combative style are liabilities for the party in future elections. They advocate for a return to Reagan-era conservatism, with an emphasis on free markets, strong national defense, and traditional family values, while distancing themselves from Trump's personal brand of politics.

In contrast, Trump loyalists within the party argue that Trumpism is the future of the GOP, citing his ability to energize the base and bring new voters into the fold. They view Trump's approach as a necessary response to what they perceive as a corrupt political establishment and a biased media landscape. Figures like Marjorie Taylor Greene, Matt Gaetz, and Paul Gosar have positioned themselves as champions of Trump's agenda, often clashing with establishment Republicans over issues like impeachment, foreign policy, and spending.

The internal divide came to a head during the 2021 vote to oust Liz Cheney from her position as House GOP Conference Chair, following her outspoken criticism of Trump's claims about the 2020 election. Cheney's removal was seen as a litmus test for the party's direction, with her opponents framing it as a necessary step to maintain unity, while her supporters viewed it as a suppression of dissenting voices.

The split within the GOP is not just ideological but also strategic. Trump loyalists emphasize the need to appeal to the base and focus on issues like immigration, trade, and election security, while establishment figures argue that the party must broaden its appeal to suburban voters, independents, and women to win national elections. This strategic tension will likely play a central role in the 2024 presidential primaries and shape the GOP's platform moving forward.

Despite these divisions, one thing remains clear: Trump's impact on the Republican Party is still strong. Whether or not he wins in 2024, Trumpism will likely continue to shape the party's messaging, candidate choices, and voter outreach for the foreseeable future. The debate over the GOP's direction is part of a broader discussion about the future of American conservatism and the evolving balance between populist themes and traditional values within the party.

Chapter 17: 2024 Campaign Dynamics

The 2024 presidential campaign has been marked by unprecedented challenges, with Donald Trump once again at the center of a deeply polarized political landscape. From deciding to run for a third time to facing intense media scrutiny and new security threats, Trump's campaign has been a mixture of resilience, controversy, and unexpected twists.

Trump's Decision to Run Again

Trump officially announced his 2024 presidential run in November 2023, positioning himself as the leader of the America First movement. His decision came after months of speculation and a series of rallies that hinted at a possible comeback. Despite facing two impeachments, ongoing investigations, and the aftermath of the January 6 events, Trump remained undeterred, portraying himself as a victim of political persecution and a defender of the American people.

His campaign slogan for 2024—Make America Great Again, Again—reflects both continuity with his previous campaigns and an effort to rally his base around familiar issues like border security, economic revival, and election integrity. Trump's decision to run again has been driven by strong support within the Republican base, which continues to view him as the party's most influential figure. His focus has been on energizing grassroots voters, many of whom see Trump as the only candidate capable of taking on the "corrupt establishment" in Washington.

Media Dynamics and New Strategies

From the outset, Trump's 2024 campaign has adopted a multi-pronged media strategy designed to counter both mainstream media narratives and social media restrictions. Unlike in previous campaigns, where Trump relied heavily on Twitter, the 2024 campaign has utilized Truth Social—Trump's own social media platform—as the primary tool for communication. This shift was necessitated by Trump's ban from major social platforms following the Capitol riot, though efforts to re-establish his presence on Twitter and other platforms are ongoing.

Trump's rallies have remained the central feature of his campaign strategy, with events held across key swing states like Pennsylvania, Ohio, Arizona, and Georgia. These rallies not only serve as voter outreach efforts but also as fundraising opportunities. They are often live-streamed to millions, amplifying Trump's message and maintaining direct contact with his supporters.

Despite his direct messaging, Trump continues to face significant pushback from mainstream media outlets, which have been critical of his campaign's focus on election fraud claims, immigration crackdowns, and attacks on political opponents. However, pro-Trump media outlets like Fox News, Newsmax, and One America News Network (OANN) continue to provide favorable coverage, reinforcing Trump's appeal among his core supporters. The campaign's media strategy also includes partnerships with independent podcasters and influencers, reflecting Trump's embrace of alternative media as a means to bypass traditional news filters.

Core Policy Issues: Immigration, National Security, and Economic Revival

Trump's 2024 campaign has centered on core issues that defined his previous campaigns, though they have been tailored to address current challenges:

Immigration: Trump has vowed to complete the border wall, reintroduce strict immigration measures, and end sanctuary cities. The campaign emphasizes immigration as a national security issue, citing recent increases in illegal crossings and drug trafficking as evidence of the Biden administration's failure. Trump's rallies often feature segments where he critiques the current administration's handling of the southern border, calling it a "national disgrace."

National Security: In response to the recent assassination attempts (detailed below), Trump has intensified his focus on national security, framing the incidents as evidence of a broader decline in law and order. He has promised to increase funding for law enforcement, boost intelligence capabilities, and restore "law and order" as key elements of his administration. Trump's campaign has also emphasized a strong stance on foreign policy, particularly toward China and Iran, which he describes as existential threats to American interests.

Economic Revival: Trump has pledged to bring back manufacturing jobs, reduce taxes further, and achieve energy independence. He frequently highlights the successes of his first term, citing record-low unemployment and deregulation efforts, while contrasting them with inflation and economic challenges under the Biden administration. His economic message has resonated strongly with working-class voters, particularly in swing states like Ohio, Pennsylvania, and Michigan.

Split Within the GOP and 2024 Strategy

Trump's influence on the GOP remains a double-edged sword. While he continues to dominate primary races and Republican discourse, his polarizing nature poses challenges for winning back moderate voters in swing states. Trump's campaign has adopted a "base-plus" strategy, focusing on energizing core supporters while attempting to peel away disenchanted independents and working-class Democrats with economic and national security messages.

Despite internal divisions within the GOP, Trump's hold on the party appears strong, with most candidates embracing his endorsements and echoing his core themes. His campaign for 2024 thus represents both a continuation of Trumpism and an adaptation to new political realities, driven by security threats, evolving media dynamics, and shifting voter demographics.

Chapter 18: Recent Assassination Attempts and Their Impact

The 2024 presidential campaign has become one of the most dangerous in modern American history, with three recent assassination attempts on Donald Trump's life adding an air of urgency, chaos, and violence to an already tumultuous race. These attempts have revealed not only a deeply polarized nation but also the intense risks Trump faces as he pursues a third presidential bid.

Butler, Pennsylvania – July 13, 2024: The Rally That Turned Deadly

It was a hot July afternoon in Butler, Pennsylvania, as Trump's supporters gathered at a large, open-air venue for what was expected to be a routine campaign stop. Thousands of red-capped attendees cheered as Trump took the stage. With the American flag waving behind him, Trump began his familiar rhetoric, listing his accomplishments and lambasting the current administration. But amidst the cheers, there was an ominous presence—a sniper hidden in a distant building, poised to execute a sinister plan.

The shooter, later identified as Thomas Matthew Crooks, was a 20-year-old loner from Bethel Park, PA, who had a growing fixation on political violence. Crooks had been radicalized through online forums that portrayed Trump as a figure of authoritarianism. Described as a "ghost" by those who knew him, Crooks lived a reclusive life, spending hours in front of a computer screen in his mother's basement. Investigations revealed that he had been planning the attack for weeks, studying maps of the rally venue and tracking Trump's movements through online sources.

Crooks arrived in Butler early that morning, carrying an AR-15-style rifle and positioning himself in an abandoned building with a clear line of sight to the rally stage. As Trump delivered his speech, Crooks took aim. The first shot rang out just after 6:10 p.m., grazing Trump's upper right ear. Trump staggered slightly, instinctively clutching his ear as blood trickled down his cheek. Chaos erupted as Secret Service agents immediately swarmed him, dragging him to the ground and forming a protective shield. In the crowd, people screamed and ducked for cover, unsure of where the shots were coming from.

The Secret Service's Counter Assault Team, trained for precisely such situations, identified the shooter's position within seconds. Crooks attempted to fire additional rounds but was quickly engaged and neutralized by the tactical team. As the gunfire ceased, Trump, bloodied but conscious, was heard saying, "Fight, Fight, Fight!"—a statement that would become a defining slogan for the campaign.

The aftermath was grim: Corey Comperatore, a 50-year-old former volunteer fire chief, was killed , while two others were critically injured. Donald TrumpTrump was rushed to a secure location, then to a local hospital where he received treatment for the graze wound. By 10 p.m., he was back online, posting on Truth Social: "They can try to shoot us, but they will never silence us!"

The Butler incident sent shockwaves through the nation, drawing condemnation from both sides of the political aisle. President Joe Biden called it "a heinous act," while Republican leaders portrayed it as evidence of the growing danger faced by political figures in an increasingly unstable climate

Palm Beach County, Florida – August 4, 2024: The Golf Course Breach

Just weeks after the Butler rally, another attempt unfolded, this time at Trump's private golf club in Palm Beach County, Florida. Trump was meeting with top donors and campaign strategists when Secret Service agents noticed a breach in the perimeter security.

A clearer picture is emerging of Ryan Wesley Routh, the 58-year-old suspect in an assassination attempt on former President Donald Trump. Officials say Routh aimed a high-powered rifle from the tree line of a Florida golf course where Trump was golfing on a Sunday afternoon. The FBI and U.S. Secret Service are investigating what the FBI described as an "attempted assassination of former President Trump."

Routh appeared in federal court the following morning, facing charges of possession of a firearm by a convicted felon and possession of a firearm with an obliterated serial number. If found guilty, he could face up to 20 years in prison.

Routh was reportedly armed with an AK-47-style rifle, positioned 300-500 yards away from Trump when a Secret Service agent spotted the rifle in the tree line. Palm Beach County Sheriff Ric Bradshaw confirmed that the weapon was described in a subsequent FBI affidavit as "a loaded SKS-style, 7.62x39 caliber rifle with a scope." Routh was a few holes ahead of Trump at the Trump International Golf Course in West Palm Beach, but the Secret Service clarified that he did not have a clear line of sight to the former president.

Acting Secret Service Director Ronald Rowe stated that an agent opened fire on Routh, who did not return fire. The swift response prevented any shots from being fired at Trump, averting what could have been a tragic outcome.

The incident reinforced the vulnerability of Trump's campaign venues and prompted a complete overhaul of security measures at all Trump properties, including the installation of additional barriers, electronic surveillance, and increased personnel. Trump later commented: "They won't even let me golf in peace, but we will not be stopped!"

Southern California – October 12, 2024: The Concealed Weapon Attempt

The arrest of Vem Miller, a 49-year-old Los Angeles resident, outside a Trump rally in Coachella over the weekend has sparked a firestorm of controversy and conflicting stories. Authorities claimed they thwarted an assassination attempt on the former president after finding Miller with two loaded guns near the rally site. But Miller, a media figure known for his work with the America Happens Network, tells a different story—one that raises more questions than it answers.

In a defiant phone interview, Miller insisted that he had brought the weapons solely for self-protection, citing a series of death threats linked to his investigative reporting. He was quick to label the sheriff's claims as baseless, accusing Riverside County Sheriff Chad Bianco of spinning a false narrative during a dramatic press conference. Miller's boldest move? Announcing plans to sue the county, arguing that he's being used as a political pawn to create sensational headlines and distract from the rally's significance.

The deeper question lingers: Was this arrest truly about preventing a potential attack, or is it part of a broader attempt to silence a controversial figure in conservative media? As investigators dig into Miller's background and motives, the lines between reality and conspiracy continue to blur, leaving a cloud of mystery over Coachella's scorching desert sands.

This attempt further underscored the ongoing risks surrounding Trump's campaign. In response, the Secret Service announced additional layers of security at all future events, including expanded use of metal detectors, drones, and increased coordination with local law enforcement.

The Broader Impact on Trump's Campaign

The series of assassination attempts has become a central narrative of Trump's 2024 campaign. His speeches now frequently include references to surviving these attacks, portraying him as a candidate who is willing to endure personal risks for the sake of "saving America." The phrase "Fight, Fight, Fight!" has taken on new meaning, symbolizing not only Trump's political struggle but also his literal survival against violent opposition.

Trump's supporters have responded with heightened resolve, interpreting the assassination attempts as evidence of efforts to block his return to power. Trump's base has responded with increased fervor, viewing the assassination attempts as proof that the "establishment" will stop at nothing to prevent his return to power. Donations to Trump's campaign surged after each attempt, as supporters rallied around their embattled candidate.

The attempts have also reignited debates about political violence, candidate safety, and the responsibility of political leaders to de-escalate tensions. Both Trump and Biden have condemned the attacks, though Trump has continued to emphasize the dangers he faces as a political outsider challenging the system.

Conclusion: A Campaign Defined by Danger

As the 2024 race progresses, the assassination attempts will likely remain a defining element of Trump's campaign. They serve as both a stark reminder of the personal risks of political leadership and a rallying point for Trump's supporters, who view him as a fighter in every sense of the word. The incidents have also underscored the broader climate of volatility in American politics, where rhetoric and action are increasingly intertwined, and where the stakes have never been higher.

Chapter 19: Historical Reflections on Trump's Legacy

Donald Trump's presence in American politics is nothing short of historic. As a polarizing figure who upended traditional norms, redefined conservative politics, and tested the limits of democratic institutions, Trump's legacy is one of both dramatic transformation and deep controversy. As the country braces for the outcome of the 2024 election, his role in shaping the nation's future is as prominent as ever.

This chapter explores Trump's place in history, the deep divisions in public opinion that have shaped his time in office, and the open-ended questions surrounding his influence—both on Election Night 2024 and beyond.

Analyzing Trump's Place in American History

Trump's presidency will likely be remembered as a period of political upheaval, marked by his signature populist, nationalist policies and confrontational style. Supporters herald him as a defender of the "forgotten Americans," a leader who prioritized U.S. sovereignty over globalism, bolstered national security, and revived American industry. For them, Trump's presidency was a course correction for a political system that had lost touch with everyday citizens.

Trump's tenure was marked by a mix of bold policy initiatives and significant debate. His handling of the COVID-19 pandemic, response to social justice protests, and actions surrounding January 6, 2021, drew both support and criticism. His use of social media to challenge opponents, media figures, and political rivals had a major impact on public discourse. Policies like family separation at the U.S.-Mexico border were implemented as part of a broader effort to deter illegal immigration, while the withdrawal from the Paris Climate Agreement was driven by concerns about its impact on U.S. jobs and economic competitiveness. These decisions were central to Trump's America First agenda, receiving both praise from supporters and criticism from domestic and international observers.

In historical context, comparisons to figures like Andrew Jackson and Richard Nixon are frequent. Jackson, known for his populist approach and battle against entrenched elites, redefined the presidency in a similar way. Nixon's legacy, though marred by scandal, was marked by significant achievements in foreign policy. Trump's legacy is likely to be similarly multifaceted, combining a mixture of transformative policy changes, controversies, and intense personal leadership.

The enduring question is whether Trump will be remembered primarily as a president who boldly confronted a broken system or as a leader who exacerbated societal divisions and tested the resilience of American democracy. His unique political style, characterized by rallying cries like "Make America Great Again" and "America First," set him apart from previous presidents. Trump's impact on the judiciary, with three Supreme Court appointments and hundreds of lower-court appointments, will likely shape American law for generations.

Public opinion on Trump remains sharply polarized, even as he seeks a second non-consecutive term. For many of his supporters, Trump is seen as a political savior who fought against a corrupt establishment. His rallies continue to draw enthusiastic crowds, marked by chants of "USA!" and "Lock them up!"—echoing the sentiments that first brought him to power in 2016.

Critics of Trump often portray his leadership as a departure from established norms, highlighting his skepticism of election outcomes and handling of cultural issues. Many of these critics, often aligned with the political establishment, frame the 2024 election as pivotal, suggesting that it represents a broader struggle for control over America's future direction. While they argue that Trump's influence poses risks to democratic processes, supporters see these criticisms as part of an ongoing effort to undermine Trump's candidacy and agenda.

Surveys in the lead-up to the 2024 election illustrate the stark divide. Among Republicans, Trump's approval remains over 70%, with many viewing him as the rightful leader of the GOP and a defender against what they perceive as left-wing extremism. On the other hand, Democrats overwhelmingly disapprove of Trump, citing his handling of racial issues, environmental policies, and approach to governance as key concerns. Independents remain split, with many drawn to Trump's economic policies but repelled by his personal conduct and handling of the COVID-19 pandemic.

The media landscape mirrors this polarization, with pro-Trump networks like Fox News, Newsmax, and OANN providing favorable coverage, while mainstream outlets like CNN, MSNBC, and The Washington Post often criticize his rhetoric and actions. Social media, too, remains a battleground, with Trump's presence on platforms like Truth Social amplifying his direct communication with supporters, free from mainstream media's scrutiny.

Election Night 2024: A Pivotal Moment

This is a hypothetical scenario exploring potential dynamics on Election Night 2024.

As the 2024 election unfolds, anticipation is at its peak. Trump's campaign centers on themes of national revival, border security, and economic growth, while his opponent, likely Vice President Kamala Harris, focuses on expanding healthcare, addressing climate change, and reinforcing democratic norms. The stakes are higher than ever, with Trump promising a triumphant return and Harris urging voters to "protect democracy from extremism."

The final hours of Election Day are tense. Early results in key swing states, including Pennsylvania, Florida, Arizona, and Georgia, show Trump with a slight lead, prompting optimism among his supporters. Trump's campaign releases a statement saying he has "won big," while a jubilant Trump tells supporters at Mar-a-Lago, "This is the greatest comeback in history. We've done it, folks!"

However, as the night progresses, the counting of mail-in and absentee ballots shifts momentum. Harris gains ground, particularly in cities like Philadelphia, Detroit, and Atlanta, where mail-in voting is more common. By 2 a.m., the race remains too close to call, with both campaigns preparing for potential legal challenges. Trump's advisors urge him to hold firm, while Harris's team emphasizes that "every vote must be counted."

The uncertainty leads to tensions nationwide. Trump supporters, wary of potential fraud, gather outside state capitols chanting "Stop the Steal 2.0!" Clashes erupt in some areas, complicating police efforts to maintain order. Meanwhile, Harris supporters rally in major cities, calling for all ballots to be counted and urging respect for democratic processes.

Tensions spill into the streets. Trump supporters, convinced by his earlier claims of potential fraud, gather outside state capitols, chanting slogans like "Stop the Steal 2.0!" Clashes erupt in some areas, with police struggling to maintain order. Meanwhile, Harris supporters rally in major cities, demanding that "democracy be respected" and all ballots be counted.

As days pass after Election Night, the uncertainty only deepens. Media coverage remains divided—some networks emphasize Trump's early lead, while others highlight Harris's surge in late-counted mail-in ballots. Legal teams for both candidates scramble to file lawsuits in contested states, debating issues like mail-in ballot validity, signature matches, and voter ID laws. The legal battles could stretch on for weeks, potentially requiring Supreme Court intervention, reminiscent of Bush v. Gore in 2000.

If Trump ultimately prevails, the political landscape could erupt with protests, as critics label the result illegitimate. His second term would likely feature aggressive policy shifts, including a crackdown on immigration, dismantling of Biden-era policies, and investigations into the 2020 and 2024 elections. Trump's focus on loyalty might lead to reshuffling federal agencies, judicial appointments, and potential efforts to change constitutional norms. Supporters would celebrate this as a "restoration of the republic," while opponents might fear a breakdown of democratic checks and balances.

If Harris emerges victorious after prolonged recounts and legal challenges, Trump's refusal to accept defeat could spark a crisis of legitimacy. Believing the result was fraudulent, Trump supporters might take to the streets in large numbers, risking widespread civil unrest. In response, Trump could announce plans to form a new political movement or media empire, intensifying divisions within the GOP and American society. Some of his most fervent supporters might even pursue state-level secessionist efforts, driven by a sense of alienation from the federal government.

The Future of Trump's Legacy

Regardless of the outcome, Trump's legacy will be shaped by how America navigates the aftermath of the 2024 election. Whether he is seen as a transformative leader who sparked a new era of American politics or as a divisive figure who tested the resilience of U.S. democracy will depend on the choices made by voters, political leaders, and the broader public in the months and years that follow.

If Trump wins, his influence will be felt through sweeping policy changes, new judicial appointments, and potentially a reshaping of American democracy itself. If he loses, Trumpism will remain a powerful force within the GOP, with figures like Ron DeSantis, Kari Lake, and Josh Hawley poised to carry forward his legacy.

In either case, Trump's impact on American politics is likely to endure, shaping debates over national identity, economic priorities, and the boundaries of democratic norms for generations to come. As historians look back, the 2024 election may be seen as the defining moment of Trump's legacy—an open-ended chapter in the ongoing story of American democracy.